Amazon Web Services: Migrating your .NET Enterprise Application

Evaluate your Cloud requirements and successfully migrate your .NET Enterprise application to the Amazon Web Services Platform

Rob Linton

BIRMINGHAM - MUMBAI

Amazon Web Services: Migrating your .NET Enterprise Application

First published: July 2011

Production Reference: 1150711

Published by Packt Publishing Ltd.
32 Lincoln Road
Olton
Birmingham, B27 6PA, UK.

ISBN 978-1-849681-94-0

www.packtpub.com

Cover Image by Dan Anderson (Dan@CAndersonAssociates.com)

Credits

About the Author

Rob Linton is the CTO and co-founder of Logicaltech Systalk, a successful integration company based in Melbourne, Australia.

He has been a database professional for the past 15 years, and for the five years before that, a spatial information systems professional, making him a data specialist for over 20 years.

He is a certified Security Systems ISO 27001 auditor, and for the past two years he has been working in the cloud, specializing in cloud data persistence and security.

He is a certified DBA and is proficient in both Oracle and Microsoft SQL Server, and is a past Vice President of the Oracle User Group in Melbourne, Australia.

He is also the creator of Jasondb, a cloud-based Restful database written entirely in C/C++ that resides up in the cloud on Amazon Web Services (AWS).

In his spare time he enjoys coding in C++ on his Macbook Pro and chasing his kids away from things that break relatively easily.

Acknowledgement

No book is the product of just the author – he just happens to be the one with his name on the cover.

A number of people contributed to the success of this book, and it would take more space than I have to thank each one individually.

A special shout out goes to Stephanie Moss, the Acquisition Editor at Packt, and Ben Cherian, who is the reason that this book exists.

Thank you Stephanie for believing in me and believing in my ability to produce this book, your feedback has been wonderful.

Thank you Ben, for the initial work in setting up the outline for this book, your work was invaluable.

I would also like to thank Peter, my twin brother and CEO of Systalk, for allowing the space to make this book happen. A book project of this size was inevitably going to require some flexibility in my day job, and I appreciate the flexibility he gave me to make this happen.

(I promise I'll bill more hours this year round Pete).

Also thank you to Kartikey Pandey, my development editor, and Leena Purkait, my project coordinator at Packt, you are both professional to the core.

Finally, I would like to thank the team behind Amazon Web Services, who are mostly anonymous; you are all doing a great job, keep it up.

About the Reviewers

Nimish Parmar has over seven years of solid software development experience in a wide variety of industries ranging from online video to mobile. Currently, he is working at StumbleUpon.com in the web content discovery space as a Senior Software Engineer building cutting edge applications serving millions of users every day. Nimish has an MS in Computer Science from University of Southern California, Los Angeles, California and a BE in Computer Engineering from University of Mumbai, India. He currently lives in San Francisco, California and enjoys snowboarding at Lake Tahoe in his spare time. He is also an avid football fan—both college and professional.

I would like to thank my parents Ragini and Bipinchandra for always encouraging me to reach my maximum potential and for always believing in me that I could. I owe them a debt of gratitude. And my brother Krunal for being the most awesome younger brother one can ask.

Derek Schwartz with over 16 years of experience in Information Technology has a Bachelor of Science degree in Information Technology from the University of Phoenix, and a Master of Science degree in Information Management from the W. P. Carey School of Business at Arizona State University.

He started his career as a contractor at Intel Corporation, providing desktop computer support. After several contracts at large technology companies, he advanced into server and LAN administration and further extended his skills to include system scripting and automation. This eventually led to software development of desktop and web applications. Recent interests include cloud computing infrastructure and SaaS business and application architecture.

Derek is currently employed as I.T. Systems Engineer at Rowland Constructors Group, Inc. (`http://rowlandconstructors.com/`), a construction general contractor with offices in Arizona and Texas. He also runs a small business, Bit-Smacker Digital Engineering (`http://bit-smacker.com`), which provides technical consulting services, web services, and custom software.

www.PacktPub.com

Support files, eBooks, discount offers and more

You might want to visit www.PacktPub.com for support files and downloads related to your book.

Did you know that Packt offers eBook versions of every book published, with PDF and ePub files available? You can upgrade to the eBook version at www.PacktPub.com and as a print book customer, you are entitled to a discount on the eBook copy. Get in touch with us at service@packtpub.com for more details.

At www.PacktPub.com, you can also read a collection of free technical articles, sign up for a range of free newsletters and receive exclusive discounts and offers on Packt books and eBooks.

http://PacktLib.PacktPub.com

Do you need instant solutions to your IT questions? PacktLib is Packt's online digital book library. Here, you can access, read and search across Packt's entire library of books.

Why Subscribe?

- Fully searchable across every book published by Packt
- Copy and paste, print and bookmark content
- On demand and accessible via web browser

Free Access for Packt account holders

If you have an account with Packt at www.PacktPub.com, you can use this to access PacktLib today and view nine entirely free books. Simply use your login credentials for immediate access.

Instant Updates on New Packt Books

Get notified! Find out when new books are published by following @PacktEnterprise on Twitter, or the *Packt Enterprise* Facebook page.

This book is dedicated to my wife Fiona, who loves and tolerates me, and my children Kai and Jari, without whom my life would be quite boring.

This book would not have been possible without your love, understanding and your ability to ignore me when I was locked away in the study for days on end (literally). Thank you from the bottom of my heart.

(Yes, Jari, you can smash me at Modern Warfare 2 now, and yes Kai, I know your Tyranid's pawn my Imperial Guards)

Table of Contents

Preface

Amazon Web Services is an Infrastructure as a Service (IaaS) platform in the Cloud, which businesses can take advantage of as their needs demand. The Amazon Cloud provides the enterprise with the flexibility to choose whichever solution is required to solve specific problems, ultimately reducing costs by only paying for what you use.

While enterprises understand moving their applications among infrastructure they own and manage, the differences in Amazon's infrastructure bring up specific business, legal, technical, and regulatory issues to get to grips with.

This step-by-step guide to moving your Enterprise .NET application to Amazon covers not only the concept, technical design, and strategy, but also enlightens readers about the business strategy and in-depth implementation details involved in moving an application to Amazon. You'll discover how to map your requirements against the Amazon Cloud, as well as secure and enhance your application with AWS.

This book helps readers achieve their goal of migrating a .NET Enterprise Application to the AWS cloud. It guides you through the process one step at a time with a sample enterprise application migration. After comparing the existing application with the newly migrated version, it then moves on to explain how to make the hosted application better. It covers how to leverage some of the scalability and redundancy built into the Cloud, and along the way you'll learn about all of the major AWS products like EC2, S3, and EBS.

What this book covers

Chapter 1, Understanding Amazon Web Services and Exploring Enterprise Application Models, we will look at some of the common architecture styles, and how they fit into AWS. We will also describe the sample application that we will use throughout the book to demonstrate our step-by-step migration of an enterprise .Net application to the AWS cloud. Finally, we'll take a look at some of the questions and issues that surround cloud-based offerings such as **Amazon Web Services (AWS)**.

Chapter 2, Mapping Your Enterprise Requirements against Amazon's Offerings, we will look at each of the services in AWS in more detail, including **Simple Storage Service (S3)**, **Elastic Block Store (EBS)**, **Elastic Compute (EC2)**, **Virtual Private Cloud (VPC)**, **CloudWatch**, **Elastic Load Balancer (ELB)**, and **Relational Data Store (RDS)**.

Chapter 3, Getting Started with AWS and Amazon EC2, we'll get our hands dirty and set up an actual AWS account and start our first EC2 instance. We'll also look at using the command line as well as using the AWS Web Console.

Chapter 4, How Storage Works on Amazon, we'll learn how Amazon AWS handles storage, as well as the differences between EBS and S3. We'll look at how to manage storage from the command line as well as configure the storage for our sample application.

Chapter 5, Amazon's Approach to Networking, we'll look at how Amazon manages networking as well as how to configure a network from the ground up on Amazon AWS. We'll also look at Elastic IPs, ELBs, VPCs, and CloudFront in more detail.

Chapter 6, Putting Databases in the Cloud is one of the more detailed chapters and deals with how we manage databases in AWS. Not only will we look at SQL Server and Oracle on AWS, but we'll also take a more detailed look at RDS and Simple DB.

Chapter 7, Migrating your Data and Deploying your Code, here we'll finally put it all together and implement our sample application up on AWS. By the end of this chapter you should have a working sample application up in the Cloud in AWS!

Chapter 8, Amazon's Queuing and Notification Options, we'll look at how we can improve on our standard enterprise .Net application by adding Amazon's **Simple Queue Service (SQS)** and **Simple Notification Service (SNS)** services.

Chapter 9, Monitoring and Scaling My Application, we'll see how **CloudWatch** and Amazon **Autoscaling** combine to make our application automatically scale to handle spikes in traffic and withstand failures of individual components.

Chapter 10, Testing and Maintaining the Application, we'll look at how we support our application once it is up and running in AWS. Also, how we can use some of the features of AWS to help us manage load testing, patch management, and production releases of new versions.

Appendix A, AWS Reference, we have gathered together all of the individual bits and pieces of information, which have been mentioned throughout the book, into one location. If you need to find that download link, or look at the definition of a keyword, this is where to look.

What you need for this book

The software required for this book is stated in each chapter as it is required. Instructions are given as to where the software can be downloaded as well as how to install it when it is required. A summary of the software required is detailed in the appendix.

All of the software required for this book is free of charge to download and use.

The sample application is written using Visual Studio 2010 Express and .Net 4.0 MVC.

Who this book is for

Companies that have designed, developed, and hosted applications based on the Microsoft .NET technology stack should not miss out on this book. If you are looking to expand into using the vast array of services available on the Amazon Cloud but are unsure how to proceed, then this will help to get you on your way.

Administrators or developers managing such applications should have basic experience of the platform and the web servers that they are intending to move to Amazon. No knowledge of AWS is required.

Conventions

In this book, you will find a number of styles of text that distinguish between different kinds of information. Here are some examples of these styles, and an explanation of their meaning.

Code words in text are shown as follows: "The next step is to modify the `web.config` file on WEB-03 and WEB-04 with the new configuration changes".

A block of code is set as follows:

```
<CreateQueueResponse>
<CreateQueueResult>
<QueueUrl>
https://queue.amazonaws.com/764516644405/migrate_to_aws_queue
</QueueUrl>
</CreateQueueResult>
<ResponseMetadata>
<RequestId>9a0b110a-8cb3-4c1b-98b5-32811b19062f</RequestId>
</ResponseMetadata>
</CreateQueueResponse>
```

Any command-line input or output is written as follows:

```
ec2-authorize "Web Servers" -P tcp -p 80 -s 0.0.0.0/0
```

New terms and **important words** are shown in bold. Words that you see on the screen, in menus or dialog boxes for example, appear in the text like this: "Click **Next** and add the same details that you added when you created your RDS instance".

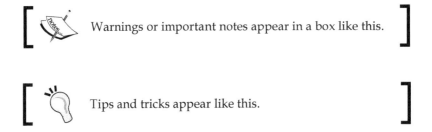

Warnings or important notes appear in a box like this.

Tips and tricks appear like this.

Reader feedback

Feedback from our readers is always welcome. Let us know what you think about this book—what you liked or may have disliked. Reader feedback is important for us to develop titles that you really get the most out of.

To send us general feedback, simply send an e-mail to feedback@packtpub.com, and mention the book title via the subject of your message.

If there is a book that you need and would like to see us publish, please send us a note in the **SUGGEST A TITLE** form on www.packtpub.com or e-mail suggest@packtpub.com.

If there is a topic that you have expertise in and you are interested in either writing or contributing to a book, see our author guide on www.packtpub.com/authors.

Customer support

Now that you are the proud owner of a Packt book, we have a number of things to help you to get the most from your purchase.

Downloading the example code

You can download the example code files for all Packt books you have purchased from your account at http://www.PacktPub.com. If you purchased this book elsewhere, you can visit http://www.PacktPub.com/support and register to have the files e-mailed directly to you.

Errata

Although we have taken every care to ensure the accuracy of our content, mistakes do happen. If you find a mistake in one of our books—maybe a mistake in the text or the code—we would be grateful if you would report this to us. By doing so, you can save other readers from frustration and help us improve subsequent versions of this book. If you find any errata, please report them by visiting http://www.packtpub.com/support, selecting your book, clicking on the **erratasubmissionform** link, and entering the details of your errata. Once your errata are verified, your submission will be accepted and the errata will be uploaded on our website, or added to any list of existing errata, under the Errata section of that title. Any existing errata can be viewed by selecting your title from http://www.packtpub.com/support.

Piracy

Piracy of copyright material on the Internet is an ongoing problem across all media. At Packt, we take the protection of our copyright and licenses very seriously. If you come across any illegal copies of our works, in any form, on the Internet, please provide us with the location address or website name immediately so that we can pursue a remedy.

Please contact us at copyright@packtpub.com with a link to the suspected pirated material.

We appreciate your help in protecting our authors, and our ability to bring you valuable content.

Questions

You can contact us at questions@packtpub.com if you are having a problem with any aspect of the book, and we will do our best to address it.

1
Understanding Amazon Web Services

In this chapter, we will be introducing you to our sample enterprise application that we will be using to demonstrate our step-by-step migration to the AWS cloud. Our sample application is not a simplified example, but a fully architected working example of an enterprise application that could be running within your organization today. As such, we have set ourselves some rather strict rules of engagement to make sure that we don't cheat!

But before we describe our sample enterprise application, and here's a spoiler, we have named it *"Waaah"* for reasons that will become obvious in a moment. We will go on to describe what AWS is, and what it is not.

We discuss some of the things you should watch out for with AWS, and discuss in general the differences between what AWS offers, and what services **Microsoft Azure** offers.

In the last part of this chapter, we take a look at the common architecture styles today, and how well they fit into cloud-based offerings such as AWS. We look at issues which are common across them all, and propose a new architecture, that addresses some of these concerns.

Finally, we take a brief look at AWS itself. We look at some of the legal issues, we give a brief technical overview, and pose two questions that you will need to find answers for before you start.

What AWS is

AWS is an **Infrastructure as a Service** (**IaaS**) provider. This means that they provide basic services such as networking and storage, but don't provide higher-level services such as application engines, or for that matter SQL Server database services. (However, they do provide some interesting database services, which we will cover later in *Chapters 8 - 10*).

A list of the services AWS provides is:

- Online Storage
- Near-line storage
- Servers (With base operating system pre-installed or with user-created images)
- Messaging services
- Alerting and monitoring
- Simple message queuing
- Database services

What AWS isn't

AWS is *not* a **Platform as a Service (PaaS)** provider or **Software as a Service (SaaS)** provider.

What are these?

PaaS

A **Platform as a Service** (**PaaS**) is a service where you do not manage the underlying infrastructure. An example of this would be Microsoft's **Azure** framework or Google's **App Engine**. The benefit of this approach is that you don't have to worry about things such as servers, networks or storage. The downside to this approach is that you have no control over how these services are integrated into your existing infrastructure, and in some cases this isn't even an option.

In this scenario, you would write your application and then deploy it into their controlled environment, letting the PaaS provider manage the underlying infrastructure.

SaaS

A **Software as a Service (SaaS)** is a service, that provides an application, rather than a framework. Examples of this would be **Microsoft Office Live** and **Salesforce.com**, that provide online mail and collaboration services. SaaS services typically are pre-written and do not provide the ability to change minor things such as themes or branding.

So why AWS

So why go with AWS when there are options out there such as Microsoft Azure, where the underlying infrastructure is managed for you?

In my opinion, the biggest reasons are **flexibility** and **control**. PaaS services effectively 'lock' you into their platform. Applications designed for a particular PaaS vendor are not transparently transportable to other PaaS vendors. This can be a feature and a curse. By locking into a particular PaaS vendor, you are able to customize your application to take advantage of those features that are PaaS-specific (such as Azure). But by the same token, if you're not happy with your PaaS provider, you have nowhere to go, and the PaaS providers know it!

By keeping your application technology agnostic, you have the flexibility to 'shop around' if you need to.

What is the biggest benefit of all?

If you don't like the Cloud model, or for some reason security changes within your company, you can bring your entire application back in-house at any time with minimal changes.

 IaaS providers such as Amazon AWS give you the opportunity to rollback your migration to the cloud at any stage and allow portability between providers.

What you should know about AWS

AWS has been around for a while now, and was one of the first IaaS providers of any size in this space. But does that mean they are the best?

Well in my opinion, yes. While they are not perfect by any means, they have one thing which other IaaS vendors cannot match, and that is **scale**. The size of the compute capacity that Amazon provides is in the order of magnitude greater to their closest rival, which means the chances of you not getting capacity from the pool when you need it is that much less. AWS is also innovating, in my opinion, faster than their closest rivals; this means that if you are using AWS, those innovations become available as soon as they are released.

What to watch out for with AWS

But AWS is not infallible.

Because AWS is the biggest, it is also the greatest in demand. This means that on occasion (rarely though) you may be denied new service requests within a particular availability region. Luckily though, your existing services will always run ok.

This means that you will still need to manage the growth of your cloud application in advance. If you think that because your application is in the cloud it is 'infinitely' scalable, then think again! Amazon — just like any other provider — still has to manage spare capacity at any given time. Too much, and Amazon is paying for capacity that will never be used, and too little, and they will run out just when you need it.

However, it is public knowledge that Amazon does not use AWS for their own bookstore. These resources are managed outside of the AWS envelope. So peak periods on the Amazon bookstore will never impact your AWS cloud applications. However, in general, Christmas will! So beware of peak periods, and manage your capacity in advance, just in case.

 Also beware of instances which may shut down or IP addresses which change unexpectedly; AWS does not guarantee that your instance will always be available or that your IP address will always remain the same. You will need to design for these eventualities (something we will address as we progress through the chapters).

Drivers of Enterprise Adoption of AWS

So what's driving you to read this book?

Well we suspect that you have heard and read a lot about the 'cloud', and you are interested in finding out how the cloud can benefit your organization. Certainly, you don't want to be left behind, and certainly the thought of getting your hands on as many servers as and when you need them is an attractive proposition.

You may be thinking of using the cloud only for development and test at this point, which is perfectly ok. This is much like how virtualization was initially used, and look how quickly that moved onto production systems.

You may have a brand new application ready for development and you find the thought of lock-in to Azure too restrictive.

But no matter what your driver is, it is now time for your enterprise to embrace cloud computing.

What application models work/don't work in AWS

While AWS is a perfect fit for some application models, for other application models it would be inappropriate. Luckily, these models are among some of the older architectures. Let's look at each of them in turn.

One-Tier

Single-tier models, or the original green screen terminals, have been around for a very long time, and in some ways have already embraced the cloud model of hosting. In this model the main server is hosted elsewhere in a data center and is accessed through terminals, usually TTY terminals or text terminals. While on the surface these would seem a perfect candidate for cloud computing, the fact of the matter is that these systems were designed to run on one single monolithic computer system. The requirement for more capacity usually requires more CPUs, RAM, or even an upgrade of the entire backend server. So while we could run these systems in the cloud, they unfortunately would be unable to take advantage of the scalability inherent in the cloud.

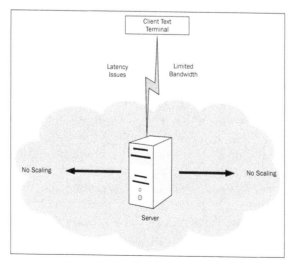

Two-Tier

Two-tier models, or the original client sever models are inappropriate for migration to the cloud. One of the biggest issues today with cloud computing is the terms **latency** and **bandwidth**. Both of these terms relate to how fast the resources in the cloud can be accessed. In this model, the client runs locally on the client's computer system, so in a cloud environment the client would be constantly communicating with the server component running in the cloud. Unless the application was specifically designed to ensure that the data transfer was limited in scope, the performance impact of this design on the user would make this a bad candidate for migration into the AWS cloud.

An example of such a system would be a **.Net** application running locally on your computer, accessing a SQL Server database located in your corporate data center.

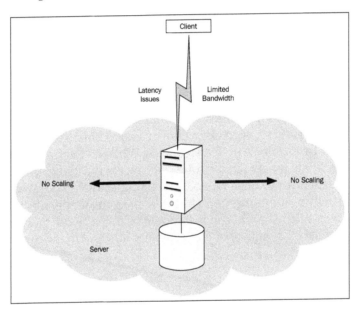

Three-Tier

Three-tier models are a grey area when it comes to the cloud. Moving only some of the components into the cloud can provide some of the same performance issues as two-tier applications. Moving all of the tiers to the cloud provides the greatest benefit. However, unless the presentation layer has been designed to minimize communication requirements, this again can be problematic. Most people take three-tier to refer to an application designed with a web server layer, an application logic layer, and a database layer, and in this specific instance of a three-tier application, the presentation layer is optimized for communication over slow or limited connections.

An example of a three-tiered system would be your local intranet or company web portal. Typically, an intranet application consists of just a web server and a database server. Moving just the database server to the cloud would result in database traffic being trafficked over the Internet connection to the cloud. Database traffic is not stateless and is verbose, which works fine on your local network, but results in frequent dropouts and errors when used on a slow or unstable connection. However, moving both the web server and the application server to the cloud results in the traffic being a stateless **HTTP**—a protocol designed specifically with the inherent unreliability of the built-in Internet.

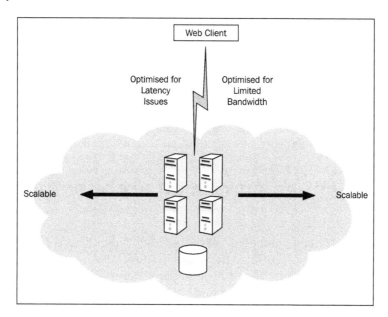

N-Tier

N-Tier models suffer from the same issues as three-tier models. Unless all of the tiers are migrated to the cloud, communication delays between the tiers will be problematic. However, as in three-tier, if n-tier is taken to refer to a web-based application in which the application logic layer is broken up into differing sublayers, then also in this specific instance, the application is well-suited for migration to the cloud. However, be wary of security implications, as the single sign on component (or tier) may never be migrated into the cloud, and as such may be the one component that slows the entire system down.

However, Amazon does provide scalable database services such as **SimpleDB**, that can be leveraged once the application has been migrated.

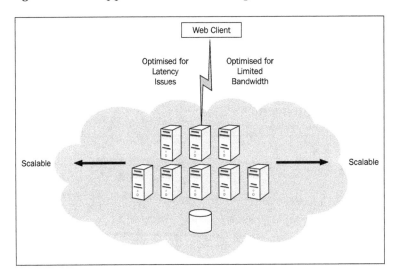

Common issues across all architecture models

One thing you would have noticed in all of the models mentioned earlier is that while some components are scalable in certain architectures, some are not. In both the three-tier and the n-tier architectures, the application servers are able to be scaled sideways. However, our database was not!

What does this mean?

Well, it means that for all the scalability that the cloud provides, there will always be limiting factors. In the case of the Microsoft platform stack, our limiting factor is that SQL Server cannot scale sideways, only up. So our scalability is effectively limited by the size of our SQL Server infrastructure. Database scaling is a hot topic at the moment, and to explain what I mean by vertical versus horizontal scaling, let's look at how data is stored in SQL Server. In SQL Server, there is a single database stored on a single server. At this point in time, it is not possible to split a SQL Server database between servers, which is what is termed horizontal scaling. Oracle, however, does limited horizontal scaling with **Oracle Real Application Clusters (RAC)**, but is effectively limited to a few servers. In general, the more horizontally scalable a database is, the greater reduction in functionality. An example of this is SimpleDB, which is highly scalable, but however, is relatively simplistic compared to SQL Server and Oracle.

So what would be an example of good cloud architecture?

A good architecture would allow for scalability at all tiers of the model, including the database tier. While this is not readily achievable using Microsoft SQL server, we can approximate this by using various techniques, which we will explain in chapters 8-10.

 While an ideal architecture involves scalability at all levels, in reality, this is rarely achieved.

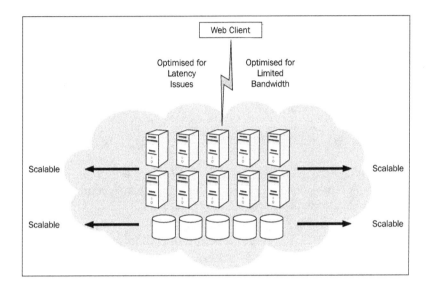

So in summary, if you have an existing web application, this is definitely a good candidate for migration to the cloud. However, bear in mind that other applications that require a high number of computing resources are also great candidates. Just be sure that whatever application you decide to migrate, you look carefully at the types of communication required between your application hosted on the cloud, and the client interface running locally in your enterprise.

If you are thinking of developing a new application, ensure that your client has a web-based frontend and that your intermediate tiers are designed to scale sideways, so that when the time comes to migrate your new application to the cloud, you will have a successful migration experience.

 Any application that is designed for the Web will usually migrate well to the AWS cloud.

Legalities of Cloud Computing

Let's take a moment to talk about some of the legalities of cloud computing. The biggest obstacle that you will encounter when moving to a cloud-computing model, is that of data security and protection.

There are some interesting things to consider here.

Firstly, let's look at how AWS is set up.

AWS hosts its servers in 'regions'. The current AWS regions are:

- US-East (Northern Virginia)
- US-West (Northern California)
- EU (Ireland)
- Asia Pacific (Singapore)

As you can see, the four regions cross three separate country boundaries.

 When provisioning a resource within the AWS cloud, Amazon guarantees that your data will never leave the geographic region in which it was initially placed.

It is unclear as to what AWS will have committed to in terms of liability. What laws apply to data stored, for instance, in Northern Virginia? The AWS contract stipulates that the State of Washington will govern the AWS Customer Agreement, however, what does this mean for your data?

At this point, Amazon is reluctant to commit to anything other than their click-through agreement (`http://aws.amazon.com/agreement`), and this will be a big stumbling block for some organizations.

However, in November 2009, AWS completed a **SAS70 Type II** audit (`http://aws.amazon.com/about-aws/whats-new/2009/11/11/aws-completes-sas70-type-ii-audit`), and as such passes the requirements for the storage and management of customer details and credit card data.

Sarbanes Oxley and HIPAA are also both areas of interest in relation to cloud services. While Amazon does briefly mention both of these in its security papers, neither is addressed directly.

If your organization deals with government or health data, please note that Amazon advises companies to obtain separate legal advice before hosting their applications within the AWS cloud.

Amazon has released a security white paper located at: `http://media.amazonwebservices.com/pdf/AWS_Security_Whitepaper.pdf`.

A brief technical overview of AWS

It's probably time we took a brief overview of how AWS is set up.

Each AWS region is broken down into availability zones.

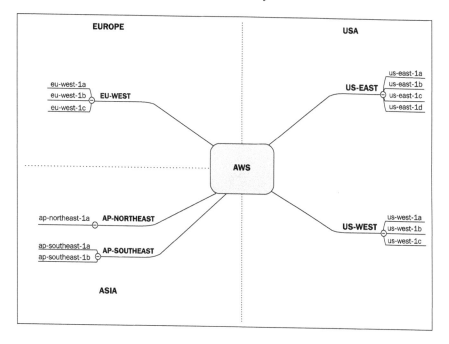

Each availability zone shares nothing with the other availability zones within the same region. The upshot of this is that if there is a service outage within a particular availability zone, servers in the other availability zones will not be affected. However, the downside of this is than availability zone-specific items such as **Elastic Block Store (EBS)** disk, cannot be made available to other availability zones within the same region.

When migrating your applications to the AWS cloud, the first decision you will need to make is to select your region, and then your availability zone.

Picking the closest geographic region will ensure the lowest latency and best performance, however, note that there are minor price differentials between regions.

Public or Virtual Private Cloud

The second decision will be whether you would like a **Public Cloud**, or a **Virtual Private Cloud (VPC)**.

A Public Cloud is a self-contained group of servers within AWS that is protected by the AWS firewall from all external connections (including those from inside your own network). The benefit of a public cloud is that AWS allows servers—that you choose—to be selectively presented to the outside world. An example of a public cloud would be the hosting of web servers, which are available to the general public.

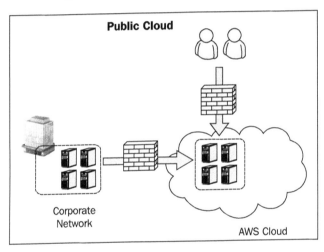

A Virtual Private Cloud (VPC) is also a self-contained group of servers within AWS; however, these servers are, for all intents and purposes, on your own internal network. The way AWS handles a VPC is significantly different to a public cloud. IP addresses are under your control, rather that AWS's. Security between the enterprise and servers in your VPC is your responsibility, and AWS security groups do not apply within your VPC.

 The exception to this is making servers in your VPC visible to the outside world.

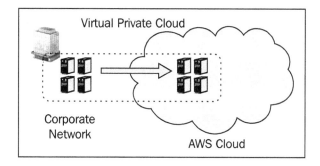

The technology behind AWS

The technology behind AWS EC2 is based around **Xen**, a hypervisor virtualization technology used within many major organizations today. Xen provides an environment that allows multiple virtual instances to run in the same hardware environment, similar to VMware. Each instance has a measure of compute units to represent CPU and memory, which is guaranteed by the underlying Xen environment.

 Currently, it is not possible to run Microsoft HyperV or VMware on an AWS EC2 instance as the instance is already virtualized.

Our sample enterprise application

Let me introduce you to our sample enterprise application, but firstly let us run through some of the rules of engagement for our sample enterprise application, and the logic and reasoning as to why we have chosen the application that we have.

Rules of engagement

- **Web-based**: The application must be web-based. While there are certainly a large number of .Net applications designed today that are still '**thick clients'**, the move by enterprises in conjunction with Microsoft is to build web-based applications. In this case, the majority of the code runs on a backend sever, with just the presentation layer running on the client machines in a web browser. So our enterprise application will embrace the new Microsoft technologies, as would be expected if this were a new application built today.

- **Good design principles**: The application must abstract the data, application, and presentation layers. Our enterprise application must adhere to good design principles as would be expected from an enterprise application.

- **Standard technologies**: Our application will use off-the-shelf Microsoft technologies. While this isn't always the case, as most enterprise applications contain some third-party technologies, in the case of this example, we wanted to be sure that we were as 'vanilla' as possible and that the technologies were freely available from the Microsoft website.

- **Browser agnostic**: Our candidate enterprise application must be browser and operating system agnostic, so no Internet Explorer-specific, or Windows-specific code on the client. We feel this is important, because even though your organization may be based around the Microsoft platform, the organizations that are your vendors and clients may not be.

- **No proprietary technologies**: No use of proprietary technologies in the browser. By that we mean no use of Flash, Silverlight or any other technology, which will limit the adoption of your cloud application, for the same reasons as mentioned in the previous point.

- **Single sign on**: Our application must support single sign on within an enterprise framework. This is mandatory for any modern enterprise application, and our cloud application is no different.

What will our sample enterprise application look like

So now that we have our rules of engagement, where does that leave us?

Well, we have a 100 percent pure Microsoft web technology stack, using no proprietary technologies in the browser, which supports single sign on and is built using good design principles.

So what will our enterprise application look like?

Our enterprise application will be a fairly typical **.ASP .Net** application with one twist. Instead of using a **.ASP Web Forms** application, we will be using a **.ASP Model View Controller** or (**MVC**) application.

 For more information on **.ASP .NET MVC** please visit the Microsoft website at `http://www.asp.net/mvc`.

There are good design reasons for choosing a **.ASP .Net MVC** application, which are as follows:

1. Firstly, an MVC style application adheres very well to good enterprise design principles, separating the data (model), application (controller), and web (view) components of the application.

2. Secondly, Microsoft is investing heavily in both **.ASP Web Forms** and MVC, and both are healthy, active communities.

3. But thirdly, and most importantly, I'm going to show why a .ASP MVC application lends itself much better to a cloud environment.

> *Chapters 8-10* show how we can take our application and make it better in the cloud!

- On the backend we are going to use **Microsoft SQL Server**. This is Microsoft's enterprise database solution and an appropriate choice for our enterprise application.

- For the application tier, we will be using **C# .NET**.

- For the presentation tier, we will be using **Microsoft's Internet Information Server (IIS)**.

- For our authentication, we are going to use **Microsoft Active Directory (AD)**.

So our application will look something like this:

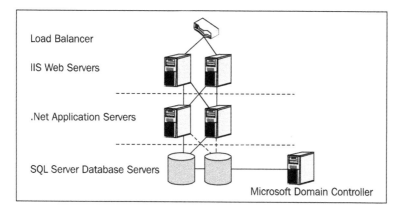

Our enterprise application will have a network load balancer, which will forward to two IIS servers. These in turn will use a redundant pair of application servers, which in turn will communicate with a SQL server database set up in a mirrored environment.

What will our sample enterprise application do

So that's the general architecture, but what will our enterprise application be called and what will it do?

Well, let's make it something that would be typically used within an organization, but something that wouldn't already be catered for by an off-the-shelf product. That rules out time-sheeting, for example.

Let's assume that our company makes software widgets for the software services industry. So our company would need some way of displaying what software services the company makes, as well as some way for customers to buy services on an on-going basis. There would need to be a way to identify clients, and to enable clients to stop their services at any time.

Let's call our company '**The Widget Company**', and let's call our application "**Widgets are always available here**" or '**Waaah**'!

 Waaah! is also the sound you will most likely be making when you get to the end of this book and discover just how much you have been missing out on by waiting so long to get on the AWS cloud!

For the purposes of this book, we will assume that the actual payment and purchasing of these widgets are handled elsewhere.

Here is a screenshot of our enterprise application Waaah:

We have a login screen, a screen that shows us all of the available products, and a screen that shows us just the products that the user has selected. (These are actually the same screen but displayed slightly differently using a filter).

Summary

Over the course of this chapter, we have looked at how AWS shapes up as a cloud provider, discussed our sample application that we will use to show step by step how to migrate to the cloud, and (briefly) had a look at how AWS is set up.

In the next chapter, we will map the features of our sample enterprise application against Amazon's offerings, and introduce in more detail the features and services available in AWS.

2
Mapping your Enterprise Requirements Against Amazon's Offerings

In this chapter, we will look at each of the offerings from AWS in more detail, and then we will map each of these against our sample application. By the end of this chapter, we will have produced an architecture for our sample application in AWS.

AWS offerings

AWS offers numerous services; during this chapter, we will look at the most common of these services. However, it should be noted that there are services offered by Amazon, which are not covered in this chapter as they do not directly relate to our enterprise application.

Over the course of this chapter, I will be referring to the **AWS EC2 console** or the **AWS console**. The AWS console can be accessed from the following location `https://console.aws.amazon.com/ec2`, and the details on accessing the console will be provided in *Chapter 3, Getting Started with AWS and Amazon EC2*.

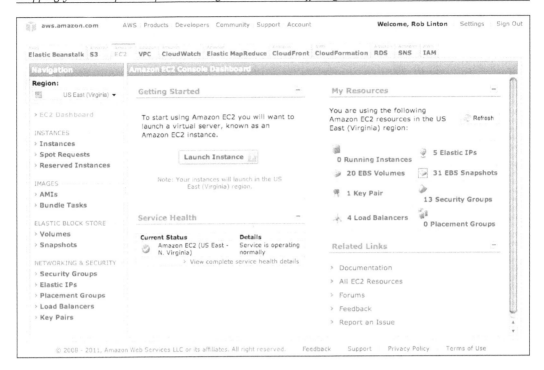

Simple Storage Service (S3)

To access the **Simple Storage Service (S3),** select the **Amazon S3** tab at the top of the AWS Console.

S3 was one of the first services provided by Amazon and is arguably the largest. S3 is at its core an object store, or in other words, a place to store things. It is not, however, a file system. You cannot access things in S3 as you would in a normal file system; instead AWS provides an API to access data stored in S3. This is one of its key strengths, but also one of its key weaknesses.

It is a strength that S3 provides an API, as other third-party providers can write applications that access this API; however, the weakness is that, by default, getting access to S3 is a multi-step process.

Some things to remember for S3 are:

1. It is not a file system and cannot be accessed like one.
2. It is slow compared to a normal file system.
3. It can, however, handle large amounts of data.
4. S3 can only be accessed through its API or a third-party product that uses this API.
5. It is a very cost-effective way of storing large amounts of data.
6. It can store data of any type.

 S3 is ideally suited for high availability, as it stores multiple copies of data in different zones.

General roles of S3 in the architecture

S3 forms a very important role in the general architecture of AWS applications, that of backup, archiving, and recovery. S3 can also be used as a staging location for migrating data across availability zones when using **Elastic Block Store Disk (EBS)**.

Using S3

To use S3, you must sign up for an account on AWS, and then add S3 as a service.

 In *Chapter 3, Getting Started with AWS and Amazon EC2*, we will be going into detail on how to create an account on AWS.

To store anything in S3, we first need to create something called a **bucket**. A bucket is a top-level object in S3 that handles security, logging, and notifications. A bucket is owned by an AWS user and can only be owned by one user.

 Please note bucket names are unique throughout AWS and cannot be shared, so use names that are unique to you, such as appending your domain name. Also, there can be at the most 100 buckets per account.

Within each bucket, objects are stored against a key that is assigned by you; however, keys must be unique within a bucket.

Each object can have individual permissions assigned against it, that are set at creation time by the bucket policy.

It is possible to list the contents of a bucket, but to do so you must provide a **prefix** and limit the number of records to be returned. A prefix can be any text, but is essentially the first part of the key that was used to store the object in the bucket.

For example, if there were a number of objects stored in S3 keyed by dates as follows:

- `/pictures/20101011/1.jpg`
- `/pictures/20101012/2.jpg`
- `/pictures/20101013/3.jpg`
- `/pictures/20101111/4.jpg`

To return a list of all of the pictures taken during October 2010, we could use the prefix '`/pictures/201010`'. To return all of the pictures we could use the prefix " or in this case '`/pictures`'.

S3 features

Data storage, availability, data consistency, and object access are important aspects of S3 which are discussed next.

Data storage

Any type of data can be stored in S3. This includes images, backup files, documents, and even executables. The data type is stored along with the object as a HTTP metadata tag. This ensures that when the object is retrieved, it is handled correctly by the client application.

It is the responsibility of the user to encrypt data prior to uploading to S3, if that is a requirement; however, if encryption has been undertaken, the content-type header will no longer represent the data type stored.

 The size limits on S3 are from one byte to five Gigabytes; if your objects are bigger than five Gigabytes, then you will need to break them up into chunks.

Availability

The availability of S3 is determined by two things, the uptime of the service and the likelihood of losing data. Both of these are measured differently for AWS S3 and you will need to be aware of this. The availability of S3 is stated as 99.9 percent, which means that the S3 service can be unavailable for up to eight hours a year and still meet AWS's **Service Level Agreement (SLA)**. So if you are using S3 for storing data, which is required to be available, live, you may find that you are unexpectedly offline for an entire day during business hours!

However, their SLA for data loss is completely different at 99.999999999 percent. This equates to losing one object every 10,000,000 years out of every 10,000 that you store. This is actually better than the reliability provided by tape backups in the past.

So when using S3 you should be thinking along the lines of near line or offline storage solutions, not online.

AWS also provides a cheaper level of redundancy called **Reduced Redundancy Storage (RRS)**, which only provides 99.99 percent for data loss. This equates to losing one object every year out of every 10,000 that you store. While this may not be acceptable for backups or archival storage, this may be perfectly acceptable for say, storing thumbnails of images.

Data consistency

Data consistency is a measure of how the redundant copies of data are kept in sync when an object is stored in S3. In some cases, getting an object directly after putting it into S3 may result in you getting the original version, not the new version.

Data that is stored in S3 has differing level of consistency depending both on the region that the data is stored in the type of call that was made to S3.

In all regions, overwriting an existing object or deleting an existing object provides only eventual consistency. This means that the delete may not happen straight away, or you may get an old version of an object.

In US-EAST, this extends to newly created objects as well, which translates to the fact that attempting to get an object that has just been newly stored in S3 may result in an **Object Not Found** error. However, all other regions provide read-after-write consistency for new object creations.

Object access

In S3, objects can be accessed via REST/SOAP/HTTP and in the case of public objects, BitTorrent. To access an object that is public in the browser, use the following syntax:

```
https://s3.amazonaws.com/<mybucket>/<key>.
```

For example, to access a public object stored in bucket 'mybucket' with the key '/pictures/20101110/1.jpg', the following URL could be used:

```
https://s3.amazonaws.com/mybucket/pictures/20101110/1.jpg.
```

To access the same public object via BitTorrent just add the **'?torrent'** parameter at the end.

For example:

```
https://s3.amazonaws.com/mybucket/pictures/20101110/1.jpg?torrent.
```

Using S3 for backup, archiving, and recovery

Now that we know a little more about S3, how do we use S3 for backup, archiving, and recovery within our application?

Well, in all cases, we will need to either custom build our own application interface to the APIs as provided by S3, or we will need to use some of the existing tools that have already been created by third parties.

In the case of backup and recovery, I would recommend using one of the many third-party tools that are available. These tools generally mask the complexities of S3 storage and are designed to allow the storage of very large files, along with the file system permissions associated with these files.

While there are costs associated with using these services as charged by these third parties, the costs of data transfer to these services is zero, as they run within the AWS cloud.

 There is no cost for data transfer to/from EC2 to S3 within the same region.

In the case of archiving, I would recommend customizing an interface to allow the incremental offloading of data over time automatically and directly from your database application, as there are currently no tools generally available for this task.

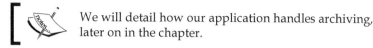

> We will detail how our application handles archiving, later on in the chapter.

Elastic Compute Cloud (EC2)

To access the **Elastic Compute Cloud (EC2)** functionality, access the **Amazon EC2** table in the **AWS Console**.

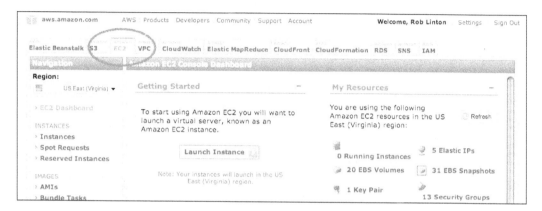

Elastic Compute Cloud (EC2) is the engine room of AWS. This is where your servers will operate and run on a day-to-day basis. However, the 'elastic' in EC2 is there for a reason. EC2 is much more than just a bunch of servers! EC2 provides 'resizable compute capacity', or in other words can scale tremendously depending on your capacity requirements at a particular point in time.

EC2 provides the ability to start and stop multiple servers from a single server image, as well as modifying the number of these instances dynamically.

However, there have been some significant differences in the past on how this is implemented, which requires some up-front planning on how you will use the EC2 environment.

General roles of EC2 in the architecture

EC2 is the backbone of the architecture where your servers are implemented. EC2 will not only run your servers but will manage the capacity that they produce.

Using EC2

To start using EC2 you must start with an EC2 **'bundle'** or **Amazon Machine Image (AMI).** Both Amazon and third parties such as RightScale and IBM provide images. For this project, we will be using the default Windows Server Basic AMIs provided by AWS.

Each AMI is a starting point for your instance. Once you have started your Windows instance, you may need to wait up to 15 minutes for AWS to generate your password, so be patient, before you can log on using **Remote Desktop Protocol (RDP)**.

Once your instance has started and you have RDP'd to it, you now have access to install any software that you need onto this instance. But beware, if you fail to create another bundle from your running instance — which you can use to start it next time — then all of your changes will be lost!

 Think of Images as snapshots of your running server. You must start your server from a snapshot.

This is the major difference between standard instances in EC2 and the servers, which you have been familiar with up to now. When installing software onto a server that exists in your own server room, the software tends to remain installed. If you install software on an Amazon EC2 instance, your software (and data) will disappear when your instance is **'terminated'**.

However, recently Amazon has introduced the concept of persistent EC2 images. These are AMIs, which are created on **Elastic Block Store (EBS)** disk. In this specific instance, changes made to the image are persisted when you **'stop'** the image. However, if you terminate the image, the changes are lost.

In fact, now there are two types of EC2 AMIs, those where the root device is based on EBS, and those where the root device is based on the S3 instance store.

Features of EC2

Here are some things you should know about EC2.

Starting instances

AWS provides a number of Windows AMIs to start from in the **Quick Start** section of the **Request Instances Wizard**.

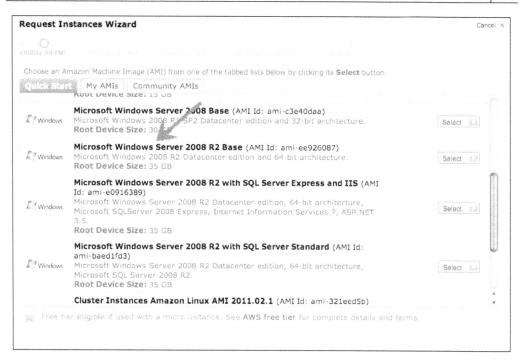

The default AMI that we will be using, and that most people will use at the time of writing, is ami-ee926087, a 64-bit instance of Windows Server 2008 R2 (Datacenter Edition). This is an EBS or persistent AMI, so will persist changes across machine stops and starts.

 AMIs change on a regular basis as they are updated, so remember to keep up-to-date with the latest AMI for your type of EC2 instance.

Typically, your instance will take from two-to-ten minutes to start up, and by default you are limited to 20 instances per account unless you have completed an 'Amazon EC2 Request Form' located at http://aws.amazon.com/contact-us/ec2-request.

Accessing instances after they have been started

When starting an instance from an AMI, you will be asked a number of questions, one of which is the Key Pair that will be used to start the instance. A **Key Pair** is a public/private key, which is used by AWS to secure your instance when it is starting. You can create your initial Key Pair in the AWS EC2 Console. After your instance has started, you use this Key Pair to gain access to the administrator password of your instance. Because you specified the same Key Pair when it was started, only this Key Pair can be used to decrypt the administrator password.

You will also be asked to supply a security zone, with the option of using the default one, which allows RDP only externally.

 This combination of Key Pairs and Security Zones work together to ensure that access to your new instance is restricted to just yourself.

When each instance starts, it is automatically allocated a public IP address and externally accessible DNS name. An example of one of these is:

ec2-175-41-165-223.ap-southeast-1.compute.amazonaws.com

As you can see, this is based on the publically accessible IP address of your newly created instance, and includes the availability zone and region that your instance is running in.

You can also allocate a static IP address using an AWS '**Elastic IP'**, which, once allocated, remains the same and can be used as a permanent access point to your instance once started.

So with the publically accessible DNS name in addition to the Administrator password, you will now have everything you need to RDP to your new instance.

Types of hardware to run an instance on

AWS allows you to run your AMIs on a range of differing hardware configurations. All configurations are measured in Elastic Compute (EC) units. An EC unit is roughly equivalent to 1.0-1.2GHz 2007 Opteron or 2007 Xeon Processor.

A full description of each of the Instance types is described next:

Types of billed instances

Instances are billed differently depending on how the instance is reserved and whether it is a spot instance. Also instances are billed differently in each geographic region.

A **Reserved Instance** is an instance that you reserve up front for a fixed term. This is in effect letting Amazon know that you will be requiring this instance size for a fixed period. This in turn allows Amazon to manage the capacity of its backend server farm more effectively, and ultimately reduce costs, which they then pass on to you.

A reserved instance has a one off cost up front, and then also incurs a usage charge. However, the usage charge in addition to the upfront cost over the lifetime of the fixed period is substantially cheaper than running a non-reserved instance over the same period of time.

For example:

As of November 2010, the non-reserved instance cost of a large instance in US-EAST was 0.48 dollar/hour for a Windows instance.

For a reserved instance, the cost was 0.20 dollar/hour, with an upfront cost of 910 dollars.

Calculating that out over a one-year term we have:

Un-Reserved instance or On-Demand Instance:

8760 hours * $0.48 = $4,204.80

For a Reserved Instance over a fixed one-year period:

(8760 hours * $0.20) + $910 = $2,662

This equates to a 37 percent saving!

Spot instances on the other hand are almost the complete opposite of reserved instances. Spot instances allow you to set a price and the number of instances you would like to run at that price, and if there is spare capacity and the spot price per hour falls below your set price, your instances will start and run. When the spot price rises above your set price, your spot instances will automatically stop.

To give you an example of spot prices, here is the average spot price for the past three months for a Windows micro instance.

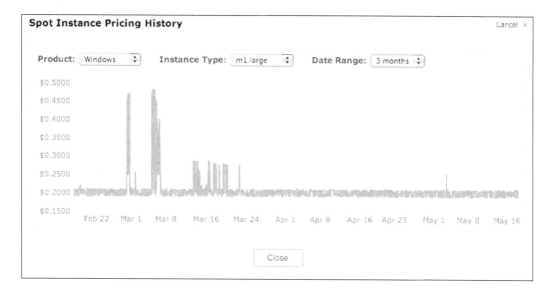

Spot pricing is based on the availability of resources within the AWS pool, and is a creative way for Amazon to encourage the use of spare capacity without being committed to providing that spare capacity in times of peak usage.

Billing and data transfer

Within the AWS ecosystem, billing does not occur for data transfer within the same region. What this effectively means is that any data transfer between EC2 and S3 is free, as well as transfer between EC2 instances within the same region.

Effectively this means that your application does not need to take into account bandwidth charges between the various components of your application. However, transfer between geographic regions does incur a cost, as does transfer in and out of EC2 to the general Internet.

The pricing in AWS is complex and is almost always based on usage. For example, for EC2 instances, there is an instance cost and an Internet data transfer cost. This means, not only do you pay for your instance, but you also pay for how much data is transferred to/from it from the public Internet. The good news is that the data transfer pricing is very reasonable and quite low, often equating to less than 10 percent of the cost of running your infrastructure on AWS.

Elastic IP addresses

Elastic IP addresses allow a persistent IP address to be allocated to an instance. It is necessary to do this as the IP address of an instance will change each time it is stopped and started. Each AWS account is limited to five Elastic IP addresses at a time; however, using the support form located at `http://aws.amazon.com/contact-us/eip_limit_request` you can modify this.

 If you are not using an Elastic IP address, you are charged; so release unused IP addresses if you can.

When mapping a permanent IP address to an instance, the mapping process can take up to ten minutes to complete, so using Elastic IP Addresses may not be a good failover solution if outage time is an issue. If that is the case, consider using an **Elastic Load Balancer (ELB).**

Instance types

Amazon EC2 has a great range of instance types and configurations to choose from. They range from instances that are tiny in size and provide less than one EC2 compute unit and only 600 MB of memory, to massive instances that have 68 GB of memory and 26 EC2 compute units. Amazon has also recently added cluster compute instances, which are instances connected via high speed interconnects and have high relative EC2 compute units, and cluster GPU instances, which provide general purpose graphics processing units.

Standard instances

Standard instances are the workhorse instances of EC2 and are used for general processing tasks. They provide a generalized combination of CPU, network, and memory resources and are well-suited to most general applications.

Standard instances guarantee that the specified resources remain constant during the lifetime of the instance.

There are three standard instance types in EC2:

Small instance (m1.small) • 1.7 GB Memory • 1 EC2 Compute Unit • 160 GB local disk storage • 32-bit only • I/O performance: Moderate	Small instances cost around 1,000 dollars per year to run and are a good choice for tasks, such as web servers.
Large instance (m1.large) • 7.5 GB Memory • 4 EC2 Compute Units • 850 GB local disk storage • 64-bit • I/O performance: High	Large instances cost around 3,000 dollars per year to run and are a good choice for application servers and small database servers.
Extra large instance (m1.xlarge) • 15 GB memory • 8 EC2 Compute Units • 1,690 GB local disk storage • 64-bit • I/O performance: High	Extra large instances cost around 8,000 dollars per year to run and are a good choice for moderate database servers.

Micro instances

Micro instances are different from standard instances, in that, while they generally provide fewer resources than a standard small instance, in some instances they can provide up to two EC2 compute units in bursts. So unlike standard instances, the amount of capacity that micro instances provide, while set at a basic minimal level, can scale upwards when capacity is available.

However, it is Amazon that determines when such capacity is available.

Also, it is important to note that micro instances only provide EBS (or persistent) disk as an option, which means that the state of the hard disk will be preserved between the start/stop events.

Micro instance (t1.micro) • 613 MB memory • Up to 2 EC2 compute units (for short bursts) • 30 GB local disk storage • 64-bit • I/O performance: Low	Micro instances cost around 260 dollars per year to run and are well-suited as worker agents or background processing tasks. They are also well-suited as development and test servers, or servers that are used for management or maintenance tasks.

High memory instances

High memory instances provide comparatively higher memory than standard instances provide for the same CPU resources. High memory instances are targeted at heavy use database servers or memory caching applications.

High-memory extra large instance (m2.xlarge) • 17.1 GB memory • 6.5 EC2 compute units • 420 GB local disk storage • 64-bit • I/O performance: Moderate	High-memory extra large instances cost around 5,400 dollars per year to run.

High-memory double extra large instance (m2.2xlarge)	High-memory double extra large instances cost around 10,800 dollars per year to run.
• 34.2 GB memory • 13 EC2 compute units • 850 GB local storage • 64-bit • I/O performance: High	
High-memory quadruple extra large instance (m2.4xlarge)	High-memory quadruple extra large instances cost around 21,700 dollars per year to run.
• 68.4 GB memory • 26 EC2 compute units • 850 GB local storage • 64-bit • I/O performance: High	

High-CPU instances

High-CPU instances provide comparatively higher CPU resources than standard instances provide. High CPU instances are targeted at CPU-intensive application servers.

High-CPU medium instance (c1.medium)	High-CPU medium instances cost around 2,500 dollars per year to run.
• 1.7 GB memory • 5 EC2 compute units • 350 GB local disk storage • 32-bit • I/O performance: Moderate	
High-CPU extra large instance (c1.xlarge)	High-CPU extra large instances cost around 10,200 dollars per year to run.
• 7 GB memory • 20 EC2 compute units • 1690 GB local storage • 64-bit • I/O performance: High	

Cluster compute instances

Cluster compute instances provide both high network throughput and high CPU resources, making them suitable for **High Performance Compute (HPC)** clusters. These instances are connected with high speed network interconnects.

 Cluster compute instances do not support Windows at this time.

Cluster compute quadruple extra large Instance (cc1.4xlarge)	Cluster compute quadruple extra large instances cost around 14,000 dollars per year to run.
<ul><li>23 GB memory</li><li>33.5 EC2 compute units</li><li>1,690 GB local disk storage</li><li>64-bit</li><li>I/O performance: Very high (10 Gigabit Ethernet)</li></ul>	

Cluster GPU instances

Cluster GPU instances provide high network throughput, high CPU resources and in addition provide 2x high performance GPUs making them suitable for High Performance Compute (HPC) clusters devoted to intensive graphics processing. These instances are connected with high speed network interconnects.

 Cluster GPU Instances do not support Windows at this time.

Cluster GPU quadruple extra large instance (cg1.4xlarge)	Cluster GPU quadruple extra large instances cost around 18,300 dollars per year to run.
<ul><li>22 GB memory</li><li>33.5 EC2 compute units</li><li>2 x NVIDEA Tesla "Fermi" M2050 GPUs</li><li>1,690 GB local disk storage</li><li>64-bit</li><li>I/O performance: Very High (10 Gigabit Ethernet)</li></ul>	

Putting these instances in perspective

To put all of these instances in perspective, here is a graph where I have shown all of the instance types with their comparative CPU and memory versus their cost.

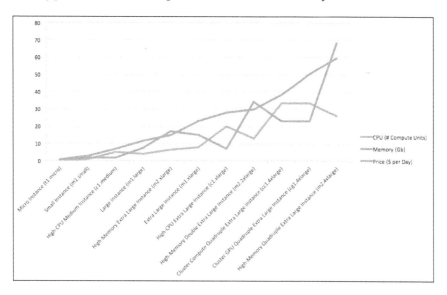

As you can see, Amazon has done a good job of balancing features and performance between the various instances, and their relative costs.

Elastic Block Store (EBS)

The **Elastic Block Store (EBS)** functionality is accessed from the **Amazon EC2** tab, and then via the **Volumes** link in the Navigation pane.

Elastic Block Store (EBS) is the disk storage system for AWS and operates similarly to an external **Storage Area Network (SAN)** in a typical data center. EBS is a system that enables EC2 instances to access disks, which are configured, created, and managed externally to each EC2 instance.

EBS disks can be created independently of an EC2 instance and can be moved between EC2 instances at will.

In fact, if EC2 is the engine of AWS, you could consider EBS to be the fuel tank, holding all the resources for applications running on EC2.

EBS disks are a powerful feature of AWS and hold persistent data. This means that any data stored on an EBS volume will persist after an EC2 instance has been stopped or terminated.

EBS disk is also faster than the instance disk associated with an EC2 running instance if the instance uses the S3 instance store.

EBS volumes can be created from within the AWS console and can be created any size between one GB to one TB in size.

Some things to know about EBS

EBS volumes are restricted to the region and availability zone in which they are created. This effectively means that if you create an EBS volume in US region east, availability zone 1a (us-east-1a), this EBS volume will not be available in US region east, availability zone 1b (us-east-1b).

However, EBS volumes can be **snapshotted**. This feature allows us to take a snapshot of a running and attached EBS volume and store it to S3.

 However, the S3 storage location for EBS snapshots cannot be accessed directly.

Once the snapshot has been completed, a new volume can be created from this snapshot, and in this case, in any availability zone within the current region. So using the process of snapshots, EBS volumes can be migrated between availability zones; however, they cannot me to be migrated directly between regions.

EBS volumes cannot be mounted on multiple EC2 instances; however, EC2 instances may have multiple EBS volumes mounted.

Some key differences between EBS and S3 are:

- S3 volumes cannot be mounted directly and are typically used for near-line storage applications, such as backups, second tier storage of data, and archives.

- EBS volumes are considered online storage and can be used to store datafiles for running databases and any other normal task that file systems are required for.

Attaching a two TB of disk to an EC2 instance

Because there is a one TB limit on EBS volumes, to add a two TB disk to a running EC2 instance, you would need to do the following:

1. Create two separate EBS volumes, each volume one TB in size.

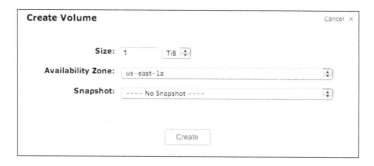

2. Add these separately to the running EC2 instance by selecting **Attach Volume** from the list.

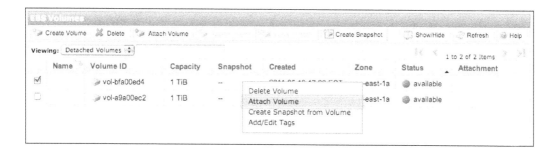

3. In the Windows running instance in Disk Manager these will appear as separate uninitialized disks. Initialize these volumes and create a new striped volume and assign a disk letter.

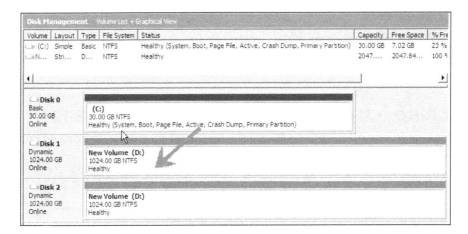

 Please note, currently there is a limit of 11 EBS disks that can be attached to a running Windows EC2 instance.

Security Groups

The **Security Group** functionality is accessed from the **Amazon EC2** tab, and then via the **Security Groups** link in the Navigation pane.

Security groups define the access policies for new EC2 instances. Every instance started is required to exist in a security group. However, a security group does not provide firewall security to a group of servers (the word "group" is somewhat misleading in this context). Instead a security group is similar to a personal firewall, in that the security policies defined within a security group apply to each server individually within that group. Multiple servers defined in the same group do not share subnets and do not have unrestricted access to each other.

When starting Windows instances, AWS provides a group called "**quick-start-1**", which opens the single port 3389 for RDP. This allows you to access your instance initially. However, you should be aware that everyone else could also access this port, as the quick-start-1 security group does not restrict source IP addresses.

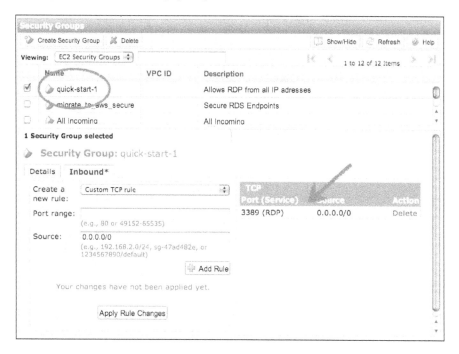

It is recommended that you create your own security group prior to launching any EC2 instances, and that you restrict both the ports and the source IP address ranges to only give you access.

 Please note, security groups cannot be changed once an EC2 instance is launched.

Implementing an example security group for a web application

In a standard website, there are often multiple security zones protected by separate physical firewalls. In the following diagram, the red dotted lines represent the locations of the firewalls.

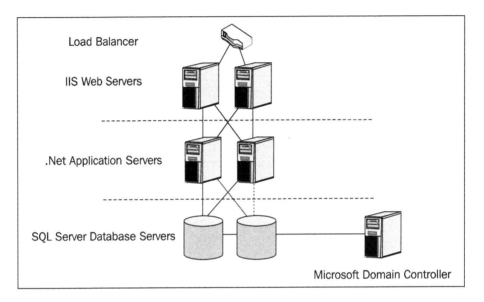

Within the AWS ecosystem, this can be achieved by the following security group configuration:

Management security group

The management security group allows access from a specified IP address to all servers in the management group via RDP. For security reasons, we do not allow access to all the servers within our architecture directly from the Internet, but instead allow access to only the management servers directly. Please note that the IP address is blacked out in the following screenshot for security reasons.

> Remember to set the netmask to **/32**, as this restricts access to a single IP address as the source address.

Web server security group

The web server security group allows access to the web servers via ports 80 and 443 only, from all source IP addresses. However, servers who are part of the management security group are also allowed access; this ensures that only web traffic can access these servers and any connections from the management server.

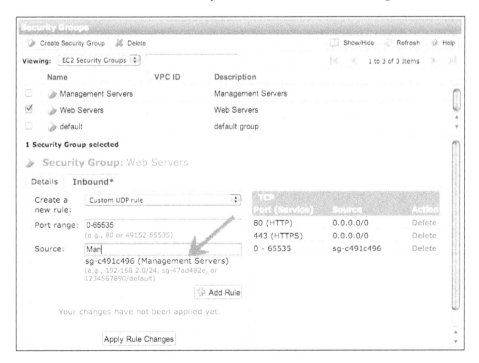

Application server security group

The application server security group allows access from the web servers and the management group.

This ensures that access to these servers can only be via the web servers or the management console.

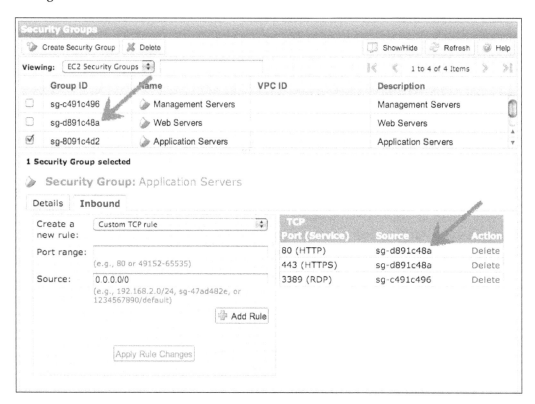

Database server security group

The database server security group is similar to the application server security group, in that it only allows access from the application server layer above, and not directly from the Internet or the web servers.

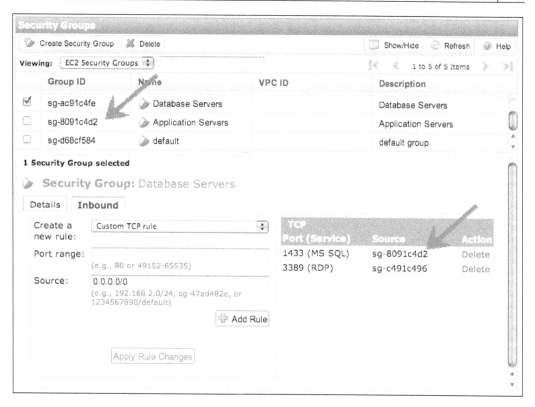

Using the AWS console tools

Because of the limitations of using the AWS GUI interface for defining security groups, you may want to use the AWS console tools to configure these. These are the commands you would most likely use to configure the same groups above, but limit the port ranges between the groups.

```
ec2-authorize "Web Servers" -P tcp -p 80 -s 0.0.0.0/0

ec2-authorize "Web Servers" -P tcp -p 443 -s 0.0.0.0/0

ec2-authorize "Web Servers" -P tcp -p 3389 -o "Management Servers"

ec2-authorize "Application Servers" -P tcp -p <Application port> -o "Web
    Servers"

ec2-authorize "Application Servers" -P tcp -p 3389 -o "Management
    Servers"

ec2-authorize "Database Servers" -P tcp -p <database port> -o
    "Application Servers"

ec2-authorize "Database Servers" -P tcp -p 3389 -o "Management Servers"
```

Virtual Private Cloud (VPC)

The **Virtual Private Cloud (VPC)** functionality is accessed from the **Amazon VPC** tab in the **AWS Console**.

The **virtual private cloud** is a service that Amazon provides to allow enterprises to create computer resources on demand that are not accessible from the public Internet, but are accessible from their own internal network.

At this point in time some limitations exist for VPC.

1. Only EC2, EBS, and CloudWatch are available within the VPC at this time.
2. A maximum of 20 subnets are supported for each gateway.
3. A maximum of one gateway can be supported for each AWS account.
4. VPCs are currently only available for the US EAST and EU WEST regions.

Creating a VPC is straightforward and can be done from the AWS EC2 console; however, your enterprise will need to configure your firewall to allow the VPC to connect using the industry standard IPSec tunnel mode (with IKE-PSK, AES-128, HMAC-SHA-1, and PFS).

Currently, not all AWS functionality is supported within VPC, and in fact at the time of writing only EC2, EBS, and CloudWatch are supported. (http://aws.amazon. com/vpc/).

So not all enterprises will find VPC suitable in its current form; however, enterprises can still use existing AWS functionality to provide services from within AWS.

Here are some examples of configurations using security groups, which can be used to duplicate the functionality provided by VPC.

Using AWS for testing

AWS is very useful for the implementation and set up of test servers. Test server demand varies within organizations and the use of test servers in conjunction with unlimited snapshot space is a powerful tool that can be utilized to provide for unlimited test environment capacity.

To set up a test environment on AWS we need to create some beachhead servers within a management security group, and create some test servers within their own security group. What this will essentially do is only allow access to the test servers via the beachhead servers, and ensure that our test servers can all see each other without restriction — similar to them being in their own private network.

 Each of your test servers may have an IP address that will not actually be on the same subnet.

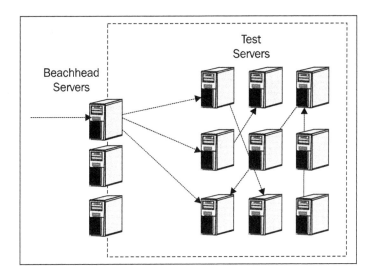

To set up this test server environment within AWS all that is required are the following two groups:

Management servers

This group will provide the access to the test servers. Because we have specified a source IP address, access to the beachhead servers will be restricted to a single source IP address, usually your corporate firewall. This group is the same as the management servers group from the previous section.

Test servers

This group is a special group designed to allow all servers in this group to access all other servers defined as part of the same group, as well as allowing access from the management servers. Create a group like this for each of the test environments that you would like to set up.

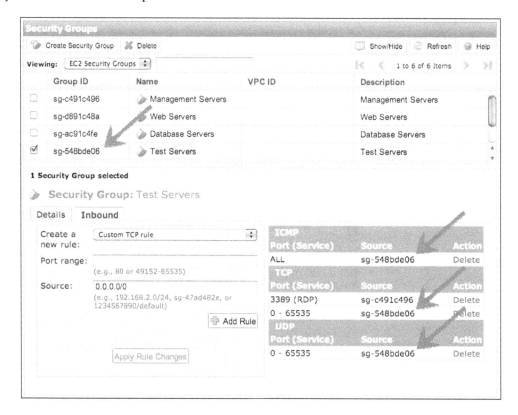

Storage servers

Having access to storage servers with unlimited capacity can be a valuable commodity within an organization, especially storage servers that have the ability to offload online storage to near-line storage (S3) as required.

It is fairly straightforward to set up a simple storage server on AWS using Microsoft Windows. To do so the architecture would look as follows:

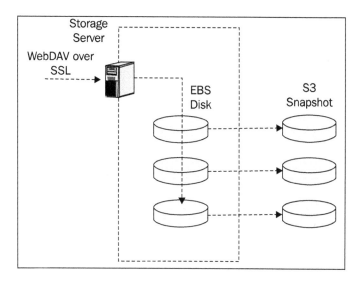

Storage server security group

To set up the previous configuration using security groups, only one security group would be required. This security group would allow only HTTPS and the RDP protocol, and would restrict access to the corporate firewall.

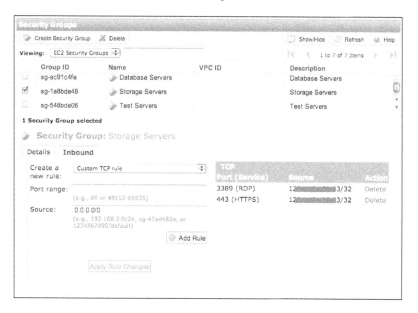

Basic CloudWatch

The basic **CloudWatch** functionality can be accessed from the **Amazon EC2** tab via the **Instances** link in the Navigation pane, and then via the **Monitoring** tab in the EC2 Instance window.

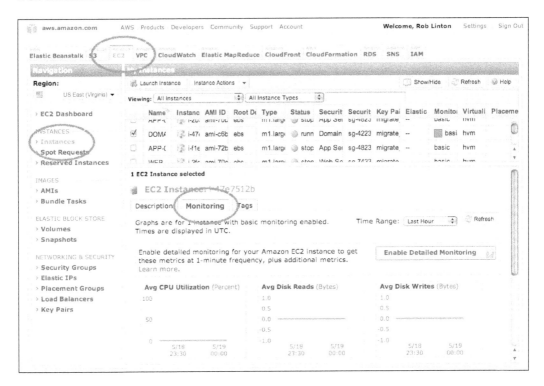

CloudWatch allows you to monitor basic metrics of your AWS components from within the AWS EC2 console. CloudWatch can be a valuable tool to provide diagnostics on performance issues, which can be accessed from a central location. CloudWatch doesn't replace **Windows Perfmon (The Microsoft performance monitoring tool)**, but works in parallel with **Perfmon** and **Windows Management Instrumentation (WMI)** counters to give a balanced overview.

CloudWatch can be enabled during instance startup or can be enabled after an instance has started from the AWS console.

The following basic statistics are supported by CloudWatch. These are collected at five minute intervals and provide the following counters:

Group	Counter
CPU	Average
Disk reads	Minimum
Disk writes	Maximum
Network in	Sum
Network out	Samples

This is an example of a graph of the Network Out data that can be displayed in the AWS console.

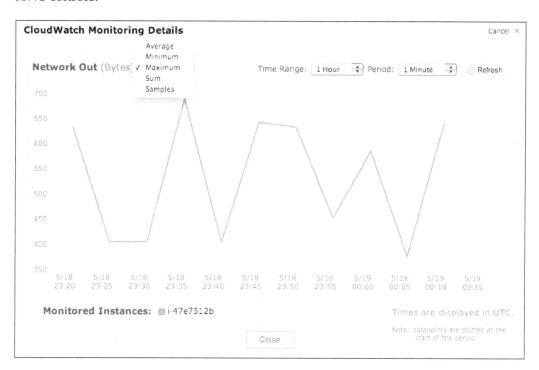

Detailed CloudWatch

Amazon has recently released a more detailed version of CloudWatch, which is now available in its own tab.

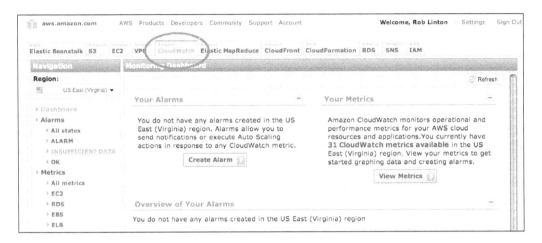

The new version of CloudWatch has a comprehensive list of metrics to choose from as well as the ability to associate alarms and notifications using Amazon SNS.

Elastic Load balancing (ELB)

Elastic Load Balancing (ELB) is an AWS service that allows incoming IP traffic to be distributed among several servers. Typically an ELB would be used to direct incoming traffic to multiple web servers in a load-balanced fashion.

Elastic Load Balancing can also be used to create a fault-tolerant architecture, with ELB capable of detecting unhealthy EC2 instances and redirecting traffic to the remaining instances on demand.

Setting up an ELB with AWS can be done within the AWS console.

Amazon Relational Database Service (RDS)

The **Amazon Relational Database Service (RDS)** may be accessed from the **Amazon RDS** tab of the **AWS Console**.

The **Amazon Relational Database Service (RDS)** provides SQL services within the AWS infrastructure using MySQL as the database engine. The RDS provides access to the full featured database engine provided by MySQL and allows full access to the database.

RDS features automatic backups, that can be retained for up to eight days. In the event that a more permanent backup is required, a snapshot can be taken of an RDS instance and stored in S3 indefinitely.

Replication and availability

RDS uses two technologies to create an available and redundant architecture. Redundancy is provided by the **Multi-AZ Deployments** option when creating an RDS instance. When this option is checked, two copies are created of your RDS instance, one in your selected availability zone, and one in an alternative availability zone. The second instance is not visible or available.

When updates or inserts occur in your RDS instance, the update is written concurrently to both instances in parallel.

When an outage occurs on the primary instance, the secondary instance is able to take over almost immediately, as it is up-to-date as of the last completed transaction.

A **Read Replica** on the other hand uses traditional MySQL technology to provide replication from the primary instance to any number of read-only secondary instances. These secondary instances can be used for reporting purposes, but will always lag behind the primary instance, and cannot be used for fail over or standby roles.

 Please note, there is currently a one TB size limit on RDS instances.

Backups and recovery

RDS instances are backed up by default in AWS, which is a good call by Amazon, as backups for databases are critical.

The configuration of your backups are to is set at RDS creation time, but can be modified at any point by modifying the running RDS instance. The default backup time is 2 a.m. in the morning and happens every night. Backups are kept by default, however for only one day.

[The maximum value that the automatic retention time can be set to is eight days; however, I recommend that this be changed as soon as the RDS instance is created.]

If you would like to clone your RDS instance or create a backup that has a longer shelf life than eight days, then you can create an RDS snapshot. An RDS snapshot creates a point in time copy of your RDS instance and stores it in S3 for as long as you would like to keep it there. Once you have a snapshot in storage, you have the option of creating a new RDS instance from it; however, you cannot restore over an existing instance.

What this effectively means is that you must first remove any existing instances of the same name before restoring to the same instance, or choosing a new name for your restored instance. This is the case both for restoring from backup, or restoring from a user-created snapshot.

Amazon Simple Notification Service (SNS)

The **Amazon Simple Notification Service (SNS)** may be accessed from the **Amazon SNS** tab of the **AWS Console**.

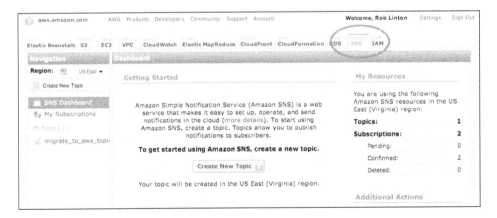

Amazon Simple Notification Service (SNS) provides event and notification services from and to the AWS framework. SNS events may be sent from AWS to inform subscribers of alerts and critical thresholds. SNS alerts can be linked to CloudWatch performance alerts, although at this point this functionality is not supported within the AWS console.

Publish and subscribe

SNS is a publish and subscribe messaging system. Systems or people subscribe to topics, in which messages are published. When a message is published to a topic, all users or applications subscribing to the topic are guaranteed delivery. There are essentially three methods by which you may subscribe to SNS:

1. **E-mail** – In which you or the application will receive an e-mail detailing the message.

2. **HTTP** – In which a web service will be called with the message as a parameter.

3. **SQS** – In which a message will be placed on a **Simple Queue Service (SQS)**.

General role in the architecture

The general role of SNS within the architecture is to provide a framework for events to be published not only to people, but also to applications. This allows communication via a push framework between application components, and provides the ability for separate application components to interact via a third-party messaging layer.

At this point in time, however, the SNS service is still young, and the functionality for accessing and connecting to it is fairly restricted. Within our sample application for instance, there will be no application of SNS.

Mapping of AWS offerings to our sample application

We have finally looked at the majority of what AWS offers, and now we can begin the process of mapping each of the functions of our sample application to the functions provided by AWS.

Let's start by breaking our sample application into infrastructure areas, which we can map to AWS infrastructure services. The following are the infrastructure services required by our sample application.

- Load balancing
- Hardware (Servers)
- Hard disk storage
- Firewall security
- Performance monitoring
- Database servers

Let's look at each of these in turn.

Load balancing

The load balancing provided by AWS ELB matches directly against the load balancing required by our sample application. However, when matching against our sample application, HTTP session cookies will need to be turned on in our ELB instance to ensure that **Session Stickiness** is in place. This ensures that sessions in progress transverse the same web server and retain their state.

Hardware (Servers)

The current hardware used in our sample application is generic Windows servers running Windows Server 2008 (Enterprise Edition). The Windows servers provided by AWS are Windows Server 2008 (Datacenter Edition); this is an upgrade to our current OS and will map directly across to EC2 EBS instances.

Hard disk storage

The current hard disk storage on the sample application will map directly across to EBS disk volumes on AWS. However, in AWS, EBS disk can scale up to 11TB per EC2 instance on demand, which was not possible in our current sample application architecture.

Firewall security

Firewall security will map to using Security Groups on AWS. No changes will be required to the sample application.

Performance monitoring

Performance monitoring will continue to be done using Windows WMI counters and Perfmon. However, the ability of AWS to provide CloudWatch will enable a new consolidated level of monitoring that was not available in the original sample application.

Database servers

Our current database servers will map directly across to the new SQL Server 2008 database servers provided by AWS. However, our current SQL Server licenses cannot be transferred to AWS. SQL Server license costs are built into the cost of running the image as provided by Amazon, and cannot be offset by previously purchased licenses.

Our database instance could also map reasonably well to RDS, although some work would be required to rework the application to talk to another database server.

Recapping our sample application's architecture

So let's recap on our sample application; as you can see from the next figure, it was a standard three-tier web application consisting of a load balancer, two web servers, two application servers, two database servers, and a domain controller.

At the beginning of this chapter, I promised a new architecture showing how our sample application would look in AWS.

Well guess what, our sample application architecture doesn't in fact change at all!

AWS provides all of the standard services that you would expect to enable the deployment of our sample application up on AWS with little or no changes.

In fact, if anything, deploying our sample application to AWS has allowed greater flexibility with storage, greater control over security, and the ability to scale the web and application layers with much more flexibility then we currently have.

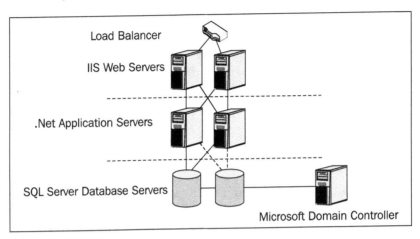

Mapping of AWS offerings to other requirements

Now that we have mapped the requirements of our sample application to AWS, let's look at the other most common enterprise requirements.

Business requirements

These are requirements that are usually determined by the business owner of an application, rather than the information technology department. However, the business often has no idea of what AWS offers and how those offerings affect them.

Business requirements fall into the following categories:

Financial requirements

Financial requirements can be budget constraints, physical resource constraints, human resource constraints, or a combination of them. To run an enterprise application within an onsite date center, there are requirements for networks, servers, data center space, and storage capacity. Often one or more of these may be in demand or at a premium, and typically there may be a lead-time to supply these resources. In my opinion, one of the greatest advantages of migrating new or existing applications to AWS is that resources restrictions are no longer a critical factor. Dynamic allocation of resources within AWS is seamless and easy. Not only are the physical resources themselves always available, the requirement for staff resources to manage and allocate those physical resources from within your own organization are also often reduced.

Functional requirements

Functionally, applications migrated to AWS should perform exactly the same as when located on-premise. However, non-functional requirements relating to performance will require analysis prior to an enterprise application being migrated to AWS.

Security, legal, and regulatory requirements

AWS may not be for all enterprises. Some enterprises require that their data reside on their own premises, or even within their own state. Amazon provides data centers at two separate locations within the United States, one location in Singapore and one location in Europe. However, Amazon does not provide data centers in each state of the United States, nor every country in Asia and Europe, and this is the core of the data security problem. There is no question that Amazon secures its data centers to best practice and has recently been accredited to SAS70 Type II and ISO27001 (**Information Security Management Systems**); however, the issue is not how secure Amazon's data centers are, but rather who holds jurisdiction over any data stored within each of Amazon's data centers?

This is a question that as a customer of AWS, you will need to ask and then answer yourself.

Summary

In this chapter, we looked at each of the offerings of AWS in more detail, and then we mapped each of these offerings against our sample application. We looked at what our sample architecture looked like and compared that to what it looked like in AWS. We were surprised to find that the architecture didn't change at all! AWS provided all of the services we required either at the same level or at a better level of offering than was provided in our original sample application. We also looked at how security and regulatory requirements may affect your decision to migrate to AWS.

In the next chapter, we will be actually getting our hands dirty and creating an account on AWS, logging in and starting an EC2 instance!

Getting Started with AWS and Amazon EC2

In this chapter, we show how to set up an AWS account and start an EC2 instance. We cover how to set up and use the command-line options and to use the AWS management console. We will also start the initial build of our sample application on AWS by creating the EC2 Instances and AMI images that we will use.

Creating your first AWS account

Well, here you are, ready to log in; create your first AWS account and get started!

AWS lives at `http://aws.amazon.com`, so browse to this location and you will be greeted with the Amazon Web Services home page. From November 1st, 2010, Amazon has provided a free usage tier, which is currently displayed prominently on the front page.

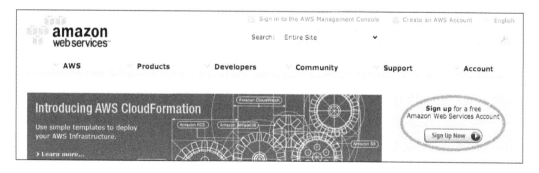

So, to get started click on the **Sign Up Now button**. You will be prompted with the Web Services Sign In screen. Enter the e-mail address that you would like to be associated with your AWS account and select **I am a new user**. When you have entered your e-mail address, click on the **Sign in using our secure server** button.

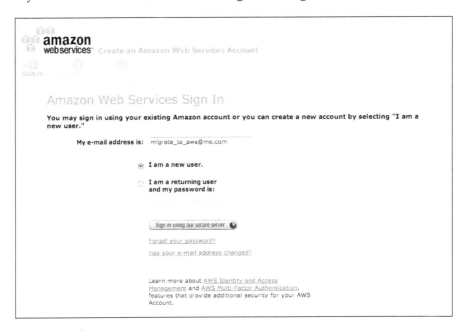

Multi-factor authentication

One of the things worth noting about this sign in screen is the **Learn more** comment at the bottom of the page, which mentions multi-factor authentication. Multi-factor authentication can be useful where organizations are required to use a more secure form of remote access. If you would like to secure your AWS account using multi-factor authentication this is now an option with AWS.

To enable this, you will need to continue and create your AWS account. After your account has been created, go to the following address `http://aws.amazon.com/mfa/#get_device` and follow the instructions for purchasing a device:

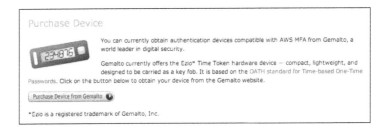

Once you have the device in hand, you'll need to log in again to enable it:

You will then be prompted with the extra dialog when signing in:

Registration and privacy details

Once you have clicked on the **Sign in using our secure server** button, you will be presented with the registration screen. Enter your full name and password that you would like to use:

Note the link to the **Privacy Notice** at the bottom of the screen. You should be aware that the privacy notice is the same privacy notice used for the `Amazon.com` bookstore and website, which essentially means that any information you provide to Amazon through AWS may be correlated to purchases made on the Amazon bookstore and website.

Fill out your contact details, agree to the **AWS Customer Agreement**, and complete the **Security Check** at the bottom of the form:

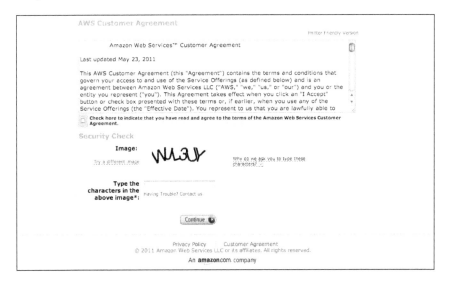

If you are successful, you will be presented with the following result:

AWS customer agreement

Please note that the AWS Customer agreement is worth reading, with the full version located at `http://aws.amazon.com/agreement`. The agreement covers a lot of ground, but a couple of sections that are worth noting are:

Section 10.2 – Your Applications, Data, and Content

This section specifically states that you are the intellectual property and proprietary rights owner of all data and applications running under this account. However, the same section specifically gives the right to Amazon to hand over your data to a regulatory body, or to provide your data at the request of a court order or subpoena.

Section 14.2 – Governing Law

This section states that by agreeing to this agreement, you are bound by the laws of the State of Washington, USA, which—read in conjunction with section 10.2— suggests that any actions that fall out of section 10.2 will be initiated from within the State of Washington.

Section 11.2 – Applications and Content

This section may concern some users as it warrants that you (as the AWS user) are solely responsible for the content and security of any data and applications running under your account. I advise that you seek advice from your company's legal department prior to creating an account, which will be used for your enterprise.

Signing in

Now that you have signed up, proceed back to the AWS home page and select the **Sign in to the AWS Management Console** link at the top of the screen.

If you have just signed in, your credentials will be already stored in a cookie locally in your browser, so you will be logged directly into the AWS Console.

The first time you log into the AWS Console, there will be a delay of around 20 seconds, depending on where you are located. During this time, your browser is downloading and caching the JavaScript required to run the AWS Console.

Initially, you will be presented with the following screen:

You will note that additional plugins may be required and that Amazon has very very nicely let you know that you do not currently have an Amazon S3 account!

The plugin that is required is **Adobe Flash,** so most likely you will already have this installed.

To use the AWS console and many other AWS services, you will need to sign up for Amazon S3 first. This is because many other AWS services use S3 to store information as part of their operation, most notably Amazon EC2.

Signing up for Amazon S3

The following are the steps to sign up for Amazon S3:

1. Clicking on the **Sign Up For Amazon S3** button will take you to an information screen, which asks you to acknowledge the pricing for Amazon S3, and enforces the entry of your credit card details, which is interesting, as the heading states that you may choose your payment method!

2. Clicking on **Continue** will require you to confirm your billing address, and once more confirm Amazon S3 pricing.

3. Please note the current limitations for free usage are as follows:

4. Once you have confirmed your subscription, you will be logged out of the AWS console. Once you have logged in again, you will be presented with the following message:

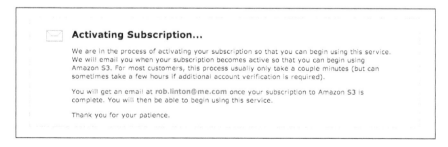

5. After a few minutes, you will receive an e-mail, which will inform you that your S3 subscription is ready.

 You will need to activate every service within AWS individually as you need them.

6. Logging into the AWS console again, you will be presented with the AWS console and the following message:

   To get started using Amazon S3, create a bucket to hold your objects.

7. To get started with EC2, we will need to create at least one bucket. However, because we cover storage in more detail in *Chapter 4, How Storage Works on Amazon* all we will be doing at the moment is creating a single bucket for the storage of your EC2 objects.

8. To start the create bucket process, click on the **Create Bucket** button in the **Buckets** sidebar:

9. You will be presented with the following dialog:

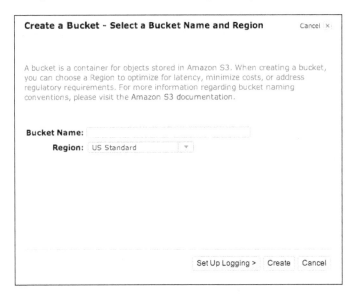

10. At this point, you will need to choose which region you will be working in for your EC2 instances. This is the first major decision that you will be required to make when setting up AWS. It is important that you choose the correct region to ensure the best experience for the users of your application. The largest region with the most servers available is the US Standard, which is located on the East coast of the United States; however, all of the other regions have multiple availability zones available for use.

 For our sample application, we will be choosing US Standard.

11. Bucket names must be unique within a region, so it is wise to choose a bucket naming system based on a domain name that you own.

For our sample application, we will be using `migrate_to_aws_01` as a bucket name, but you will need to choose a name that is unique to yourself.

Signing up for EC2

The following are the steps to sign up for EC2:

1. Once we have created our bucket we are ready to start the process of creating an EC2 account. Clicking on the **EC2** tab will bring up the following screen:

2. Once again, we will be asked to sign up for a service the first time we use it.

3. Clicking on the **Sign Up For Amazon EC2** button will start the EC2 provisioning process, and log you out of the AWS Console.

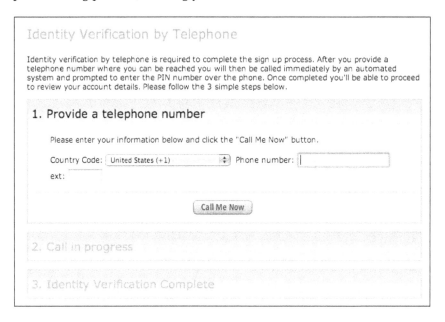

4. Logging back into the AWS Console will immediately cause the following screen to appear, requesting phone verification. Clicking on the **Call Me Now** button will trigger the following process:
   ° A call will be made to your contact phone number.
   ° A 4-digit PIN will be displayed in the **Call in progress** box.
   ° A very nice computerized voice on the other end of the phone will request that you enter the PIN displayed on your screen into the phone touchpad, or you have the option of speaking it aloud, one digit at a time.

5. Having been through this process a number of times, I recommend that you don't bother with the voice assist and just type the PIN into the keypad of your phone.

6. Once you have verified your identity, you will once again be shown a pricing screen (this time for EC2), and asked to complete the sign up.

7. Please note, if you scroll all the way to the bottom of this page (and it is a long page) you will see the billing information that you entered for S3.

8. Also on this screen, hidden away at the bottom, are the pricing details for **Simple Notification Service (SNS)** and **Virtual Private Cloud (VPC)**, which you will also be agreeing to when you click on the **Complete Sign Up** button.

9. Once you have clicked on the sign up button, you will once again be logged out of the AWS Console. On signing back into the console, you will be greeted with the following information box:

> **Activating Subscription......**
>
> We are in the process of activating your subscription so that you can begin using this service. We will email you when your subscription becomes active so that you can begin using Amazon EC2. For most customers, this process usually only take a couple minutes (but can sometimes take a few hours if additional account verification is required).
>
> You will get an email at rob.linton@me.com once your subscription to Amazon EC2 is complete. You will then be able to begin using this service.
>
> Thank you for your patience.

10. Once again, you will need to wait for the e-mail confirming the availability of your service. When I set up the account for use with this book, the wait was around 10 hours for EC2 to become active, as opposed to two minutes for S3 to become active.

11. EC2 services also provide a free usage tier as follows. Please note that the free usage tier is only available for a period of one year from the commencement of the service:

> Free Tier*
>
> As part of AWS's Free Usage Tier, new AWS customers can get started with Amazon EC2 for free. Upon sign-up, new AWS customers receive the following EC2 services each month for one year:
>
> - 750 hours of EC2 running Linux/Unix Micro instance usage
> - 750 hours of Elastic Load Balancing plus 15 GB data processing
> - 10 GB of Amazon Elastic Block Storage (EBS) plus 1 million IOs, 1 GB snapshot storage, 10,000 snapshot Get Requests and 1,000 snapshot Put Requests
> - 15 GB of bandwidth in and 15 GB of bandwidth out aggregated across all AWS services

12. Once you have access to EC2, you will be able to access the EC2 console in AWS. The console looks like this:

13. The left-hand pane gives a list of objects that you can manage, while the far right-hand pane gives a summary of the currently running resources under your account in the selected region.

 Please note that all of the information shown in the AWS console is region-specific and changing the region will change the resources you are able to manage and see in this console. For example, you can only see EU instances when the EU region is selected. The US East instances will not show up within the EU region view.

14. The middle pane gives you an option to go ahead and launch an instance, and gives the current status of the region you are currently operating in.

Starting an EC2 instance

Before we start our very first instance, we are going to create a security group that you will use to secure your instance. The security groups that your instance is a part of cannot be changed after your instance is started, so we will need to create this first.

Creating a security group

1. To create a basic security group, click on the **Security Groups** link in the left-hand **Navigation** pane, and then click on the **Create Security Group** button in the toolbar of the **Security Groups** pane on the right, then enter a **Name** and a **Description**.

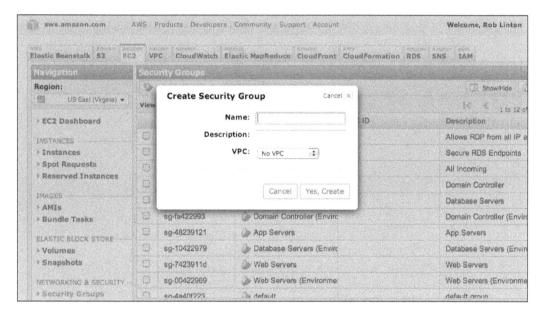

2. For your first security group, we will be creating a group whose sole purpose is to secure communications from your enterprise, directly to AWS. Type in "migrate_to_aws" as the Security Group **Name** and "Secure endpoint connection" as the **Description**. To find your enterprise's external IP address, you will need to either talk to your network administrator, or alternatively you can use an external service such as http://whatismyipaddress.com/ to determine what IP address is seen by the external web services.

3. Once you have determined your external IP address, create an RDP entry using this IP address as a Source IP. Make sure to specify /32 after the IP to indicate that only this specific IP is allowed:

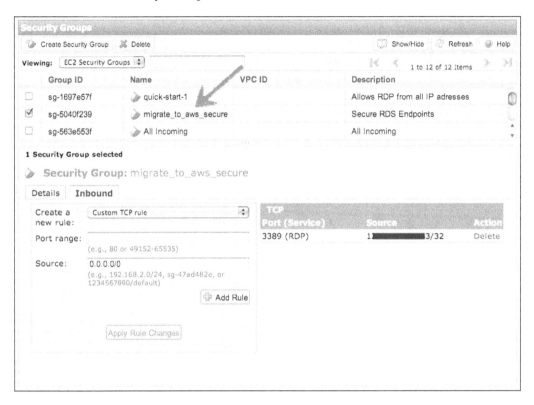

4. This new setting will only allow traffic for the source IP at the location you are currently at. If you need to RDP in from another location, you'll need to add those IPs to the "migrate_to_aws" security group.

Starting the EC2 instance

1. To start your very first EC2 instance, click on the **EC2 Dashboard** link in the left navigation page and then click the **Launch Instance** button in the middle of the screen. This will launch the **Request Instances Wizard**:

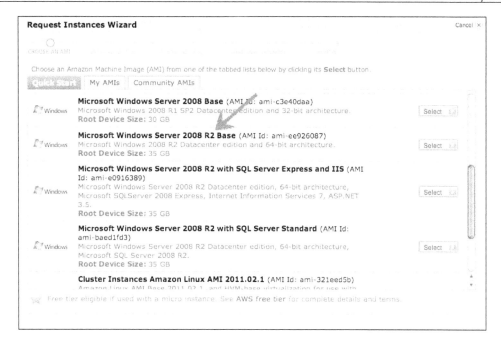

2. Scroll down to the bottom of the **Quick Start** tab and you will see an instance called **Microsoft Windows Server 2008 R2 Base**. This is the instance that will be used for most of the servers in our sample application stack. Choose the **Select** button next to the image to continue.

3. The **Amazon Machine Images (AMIs)** listed in this dialog are all created by Amazon and are base images that your new server will be based on. After selecting your base image you will be prompted with the **Availability Zone** and the **Instance Type**:

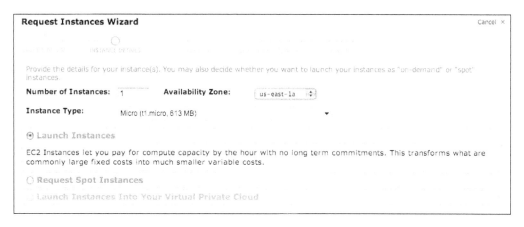

4. In this case, I have selected the **us-east-1a Availability Zone**, which is the first availability zone in the US Standard or US East region. I have also selected a **Micro** instance, which is the smallest instance that you can provision in AWS. Click on **Continue.** In the next dialog after selecting **Enable CloudWatch detailed monitoring for this instance,** click on **Continue:**

5. The next dialog enables you to choose an optional name for your server. I recommend that you fill out the name box with the role of the instance so you can easily distinguish these servers from one another:

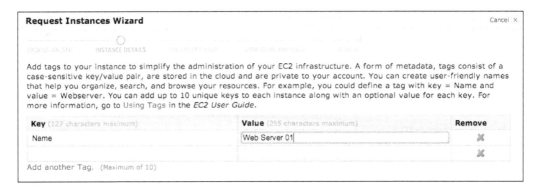

6. In this case, we have named our server **Web Server 01**. Click **Continue** and you will be requested to either **Choose from your existing Key Pairs** or to **Create a new Key Pair**. Because this is the first time we have created an instance on EC2, we will need to create a new key pair:

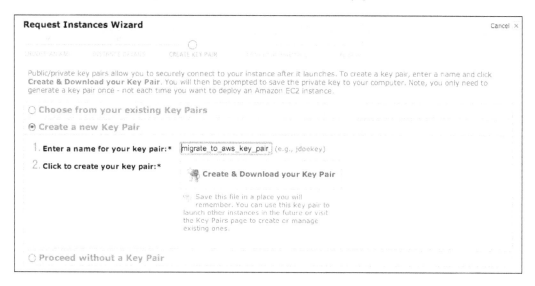

7. The key pair is a public/private key used to secure access to your new EC2 instances as they are created. When you create a new key pair, the public key is kept up in AWS, but your private key is downloaded only once, at the time of creation. It is up to you to keep your private key secure. Make sure your pop-up blocker is turned off before this step or there might be issues with the key download.

> We will see how the key pairs are used when we try to log on to our new EC2 instance.

8. Enter a name for your key pair and click on the **Create & Download your Key Pair** link in the dialog. You will be prompted to save your private key locally on your hard disk.

9. Once you have saved your key pair you will be prompted to select a security group for your new instance:

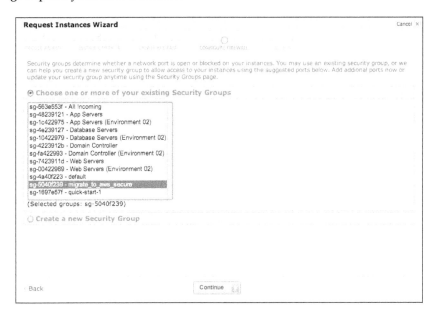

10. Select the security group that was created earlier (**migrate_to_aws_secure**) and click on **Continue** as shown in the previous screenshot. You are now ready to launch your first AWS EC2 instance!

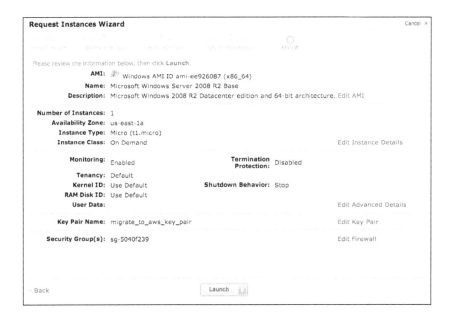

11. Your instance will take a while to launch, so be patient, but usually an instance is up and running in just a few minutes. Once the instance is up and running, you can view your instances by selecting the **Instances** link in the **Navigation** pane of the AWS Console. This is what your instance will look like when you click on the instance (in this case called Web Server 01):

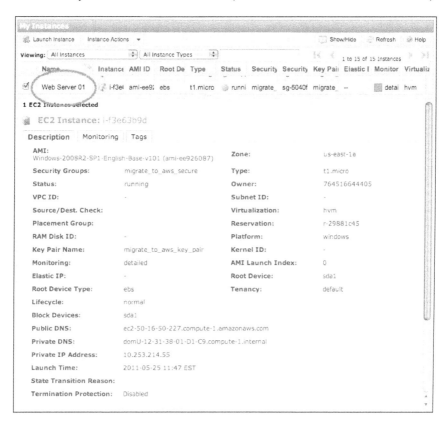

Accessing your EC2 instance

1. Now that our instance has started, to access it we will need to determine its administrator password. When our instance started, AWS created a temporary password, encrypted it with our public key and stored it in the system log for our running instance. To get the administrator password, we will need to get the encrypted version from the log and decrypt it. Luckily, AWS makes this easy for us.

 The system log can take up to 15 minutes to be available after your instance has started, so be patient.

2. To decrypt it, right-click on the running instance and select **Get Windows Admin Password**:

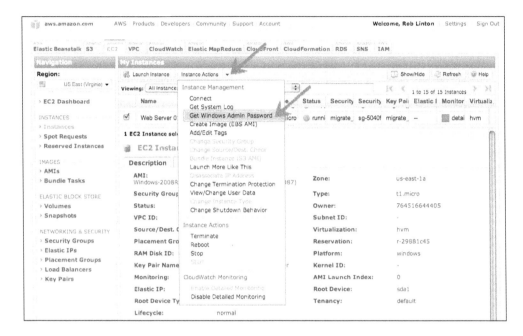

3. You will be prompted with the following dialog in which the **Encrypted Password** has been retrieved from the instance's system log and displayed along with the option to input our **Private Key**:

4. Open up the private key that you downloaded earlier and cut and paste it into the dialog, as shown in the previous screenshot. Make sure you include all the text in your private key file. Click on the **Decrypt Password** button and you will be presented with the administrator password for your running instance:

5. If the Internet Explorer prompts you to "**Stop running this script**", click **No** until the decrypted password appears.

6. At this point, you now have all of the three items required to RDP to your running instance.

   ° An administrator username (**Administrator**)

   ° The Administrator password

   ° The Public IP address

 When you RDP to your running EC2 instance, make sure you use the Public DNS entry displayed, not the Private IP address.

So congratulations!

You have just started your first Amazon EC2 instance and hopefully logged onto it.

Configuring your instance

1. Now that you have started and logged into your first EC2 instance, run Microsoft update on this instance and install your preferred virus checkers.

> We won't go into detail on this as I assume that you will have existing knowledge of how to install and configure these items.

2. Once you have updated your instance and installed your virus checkers, we are going to bundle your running instance and use it as a copy for our other instances.

3. To do this is a two-step process:

   ○ Step one is to **Sysprep** your image from within Microsoft Windows

   ○ Step two is to run the Amazon **Bundle** command

4. To run Sysprep on your running instance, go to the **Start** menu and run the EC2 Config Service application. This application has been pre-installed on to your running image and is similar to **VMware Tools**, in that, it allows you to configure certain behaviors for EC2 from within the running EC2 image.

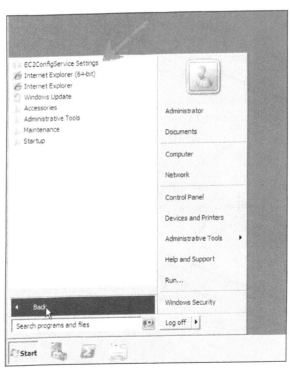

5. The EC2 Config Service has been provided primarily to configure how your Windows EC2 instance behaves within the EC2 environment. When your instance starts, there are a number of steps that are required to be executed against your EC2 instance on startup.

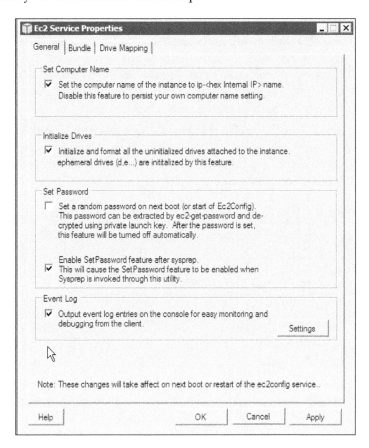

Set Computer Name: When your instance is started, by default EC2 will create a computer name, that is based on your IP address in the following format:

```
Ip<hex internal IP>
```

This means that it is possible to startup multiple copies of your AMI bundle and ensure that each of them have unique names. It is also a requirement for EC2, as EC2 must also ensure that new instances have unique names. However, it is likely that you do not want a new name allocated to your bundle, if the bundle is for a specific instance. Also, in the case of database servers and some other application servers, changing the name of your server may, in fact, break the current installation of that application or service.

For our sample application, we will be creating a separate bundle for each of our servers, but for now, leave this checked.

Initialize Drives: Because we want to control how our instance manages new drives, this checkbox should be deselected. In fact, I recommend that this checkbox always be deselected to ensure that we control this manually.

Set Password: When new instances are created from a Sysprep bundle, the administrator password needs to be reset to a new random password. This is because Sysprep wipes the original password that was in place prior to the bundle being created. Leave the checkboxes, as shown in the previous screenshot, for the **Set Password** section of the dialog.

Event Log: One of the useful things that Amazon provides is the ability to send events from the event log of our Windows instance to the instance system log as displayed by AWS. I recommend that all errors be passed into the system log, and that you select a number greater than 3:

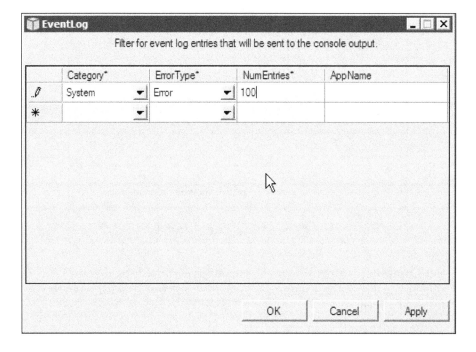

Running Sysprep: Now that we have finished the configuration of our new base EC2 instance, it is time to Sysprep it in readiness for creating our new EC2 bundle:

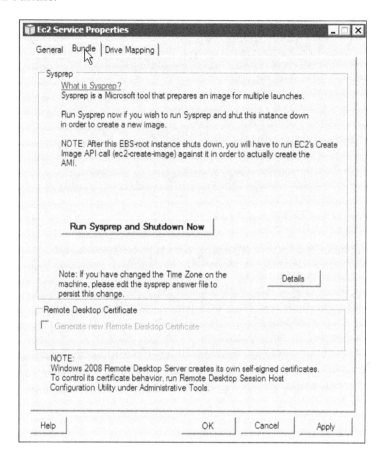

The Bundle tab shows the **Run Sysprep and Shutdown Now** button, which you will use to kick off the process.

One thing you will notice at this point is the comment referring to time zones in the Sysprep file. This is important to note. The reason for doing a Sysprep on an image is to ensure that the **System Identifier** (**SSID**) of the Windows Server is unique. **Windows Domain Controller** expects these to be different when adding servers to the domain, and it is a good practice to always ensure that these are unique.

However, the process of doing this to a running server instance removes configuration data, such as time zones and international settings. If you are not proficient at modifying the Sysprep answer file, then I recommend that you modify these settings after creating your EC2 instances from this bundle file.

6. Clicking on the **Run Sysprep and Shutdown Now** button will prompt the following dialog box:

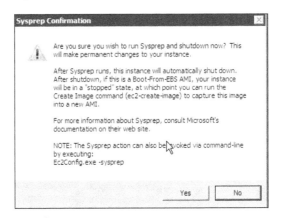

7. Click **Yes** to continue.

   The EC2 base instance will be shut down to a stopped state.

    Remember that our Windows instance is based on an EBS or persistent AMI, so stopping it does not cause it to lose its current state.

8. In the AWS Management Console, right-click on the instance and select **Create Image (EBS AMI)** from the pop-up menu. This will begin the second step of the bundling process to create your base AMI bundle:

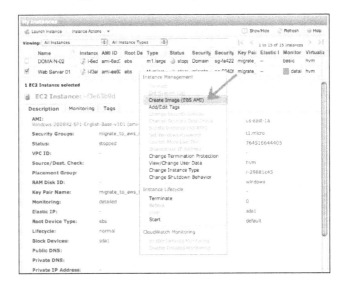

9. After selecting the menu option, you will be presented with the following dialog:

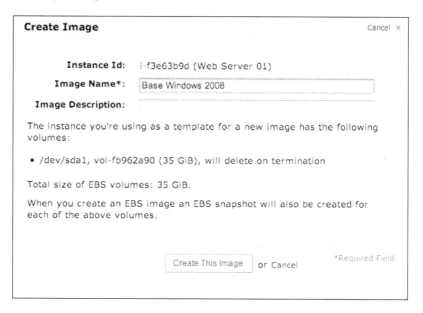

10. Enter an **Image Name** and **Image Description** and click **Create This Image**.

    Your create image request will now be added to the queue. To see the status of your image request select the **AMIs** link in the **Navigation** sidebar, your image status will be shown on the right:

Starting new EC2 instances from our base image

1. Now that we have created our base image, it's time to create our five sample application servers.

2. To do this, we are going to create new instances in EC2, except this time we will be using our base AMI as the starting AMI, rather than the AMIs which are provided in the **Quick Start** tab. To find our AMI bundle, select the **My AMIs** tab:

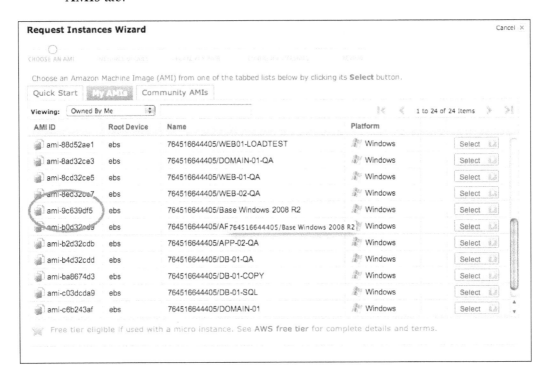

3. You will see your new AMI bundle listed with its new **AMI ID**. This **AMI ID** is unique to your new bundle and can be used to reference your AMI bundle from the command line or when searching for your AMI bundle in the AWS console.

4. Select **5** as the **Number of Instances** we would like to start. Make sure you select a specific **Availability Zone** because if you do not, these instances may be created in different availability zones depending on the resource availability:

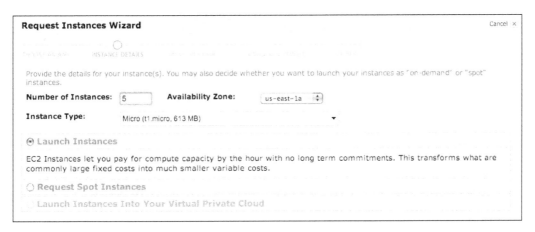

5. Use the same security groups and key pairs that you used in the previous example.

6. Once your new instances are up and running, you will see the following in your AWS console:

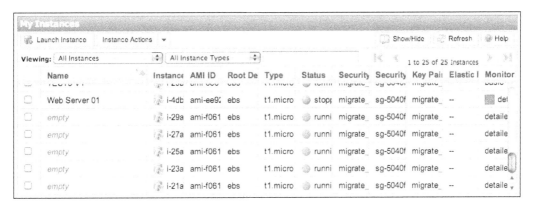

7. Note that all of the names are blank because we did not set them when they started up. So select each instance individually and give each one a name as follows:

You cannot edit a tag by clicking on the tag directly; you will need to click on the **Add/Edit Tags**.

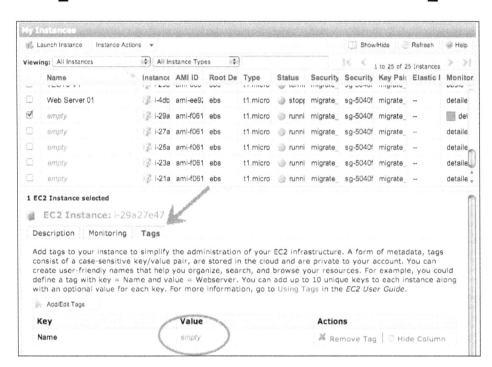

8. Here we see all of the instances, each named for the services they provide:

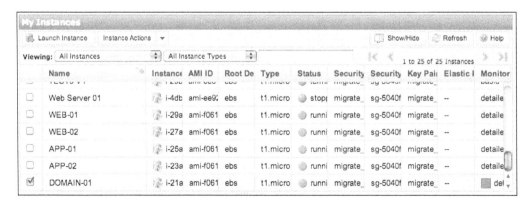

9. Now that we have our five basic EC2 instances we are going to use for our sample application, we still need to do some final configuration steps. These are:

- ° Retrieve the new Windows password by following the same steps as discussed previously for each instance.

- ° Log on to each instance and deselect the **Set Computer Name** checkbox in the **Ec2 Service Properties**:

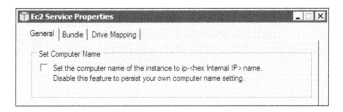

- ° Set the computer name to match our instance tag Name.

- ° If you were not confident in setting the time zone and international settings in the Sysprep answer file, then you will need to set these as well on each of the instances.

Saving your new instances as AMIs

Now that you have created the five instances that we will require for our sample application, you will need to create a separate bundled AMI for each instance. By having a saved AMI for each instance, we can change the security groups and also change the machine type that each instance is based on. When you finish, you should have the following AMIs:

Once your AMIs have been created, terminate your running instances so we can create them again from the command line, next in this chapter.

Using the command line

So far within this chapter we have been using the AWS Console to manage our EC2 Instances. However, the AWS Console provides only a subset of the full range of commands that are available to manage your AWS services. Amazon provides a rich command-line interface that allows you to manage all of your instances remotely from your own desktop.

Installing the AWS command-line tools

In Windows, there are a number of steps to install the AWS command-line tools; however, installation is straightforward and should only take a few minutes.

Installing Java

The AWS command-line tools require Java 5 or later to be installed, so go to http://www.java.com/en/download/manual.jsp#win and download Java first, if you have not already done so.

Creating a location to store your data

Create a location on your hard disk that is easy to get to, for example, C:\AWS.

Getting your security keys

1. All of the AWS command-line tools rely on the use of your X.509 certificates. By default you will not have a certificate created, so go to this address https://aws-portal.amazon.com/gp/aws/developer/account/index.html and click on the **X.509 Certificates** tab:

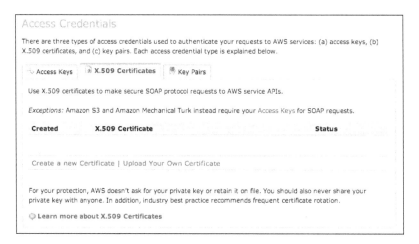

2. To create a new certificate, click on the **Create a new Certificate** link. You will be prompted with the following dialog:

 It is important to download your private key at this point, if you don't, you will not get the opportunity to do so again.

3. Store you private key in your local AWS location, for example, `C:\AWS`. Once your key is created, also download your certificate. Your certificate will appear after you have refreshed the page:

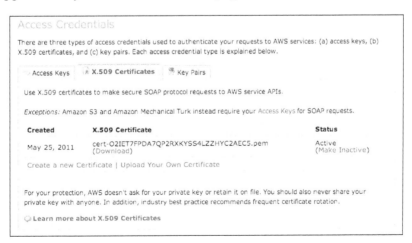

4. You should now have two files in your local AWS folder:

Name	Date modified	Type
cert-O2IET7FPDA7QP2RXKYSS4LZZHYC2AEC5.pem	25/05/2011 5:00 PM	PEM File
pk-O2IET7FPDA7QP2RXKYSS4LZZHYC2AEC5.pem	25/05/2011 5:00 PM	PEM File

 Keep these files secure, as these files provide access to your AWS account.

Downloading and installing the AWS tools

The AWS tools are located at `http://aws.amazon.com/developertools/351`. Download them to `C:\AWS` and unzip them. They will unzip into a directory similar to the following, depending on what version they are:

```
C:\AWS\ec2-api-tools\ec2-api-tools-1.3-62308
```

Creating a file to set up the AWS environment

Now that we have downloaded the tools and installed them, we now need to create a batch file that will be used to configure the environment for our AWS tools.

Create a file called `C:\AWS\aws_env.bat` and add the following commands to it:

```
set JAVA_HOME="C:\Program Files\Java\jre6"
set EC2_PRIVATE_KEY=c:\aws\pk-XUSF3YX32DTZWSBHEIENR24EANXCXUBA.pem
set EC2_CERT=c:\aws\cert-XUSF3YX32DTZWSBHEIENR24EANXCXUBA.pem
set EC2_HOME=C:\AWS\ec2-api-tools\ec2-api-tools-1.3-62308
set PATH=%PATH%;C:\AWS\ec2-api-tools\ec2-api-tools-1.3-62308\bin
```

Note that your private key and cert details will be different for your own environment and the API tools version will change based on their version number.

On 64-bit versions of Windows, the Java path would be:

```
"C:\Program Files (x86)\Java\jre6"
```

Using the command line

To run an EC2 command, startup a **Command Prompt** from the Windows **Start menu**. In the **Command Prompt**, change directory to the AWS location that you set up earlier and run the aws_env.bat file:

```
C:\AWS> aws_env
```

```
C:\Windows\system32\cmd.exe

c:\AWS>aws_env.cmd

c:\AWS>set JAVA_HOME="C:\Program Files\Java\jre6"

c:\AWS>set EC2_PRIVATE_KEY=c:\aws\pk-XUSF3YX32DTZVSBHEIENR24EANXCXUBA.pem

c:\AWS>set EC2_CERT=c:\aws\cert-XUSF3YX32DTZVSBHEIENR24EANXCXUBA.pem

c:\AWS>set EC2_HOME=C:\AWS\ec2-api-tools\ec2-api-tools-1.3-62308

c:\AWS>set PATH=C:\AWS\CloudWatch-1.0.9.5\bin;C:\AWS\AutoScaling-1.0.33.1\bin;C:\Program Files\Common Files\Microsoft Sh
\Windows\system32;C:\Windows;C:\Windows\System32\Wbem;C:\Windows\System32\WindowsPowerShell\v1.0\;C:\Program Files\Micro
Tools\Binn\;C:\Program Files\Microsoft SQL Server\100\DTS\Binn\;C:\Program Files\Microsoft SQL Server\100\Tools\Binn\VSS
\Program Files\Microsoft Visual Studio 9.0\Common7\IDE\PrivateAssemblies\;C:\Program Files\Common Files\Intuit\QBPOSSDKR
les\MySQL\MySQL Server 5.5\bin;C:\Program Files\Microsoft ASP.NET\ASP.NET Web Pages\v1.0\;C:\Program Files\Common Files
dows Live;C:\AWS\ec2-api-tools\ec2-api-tools-1.3-62308\bin;c:\aws\elb\bin;C:\AWS\ec2-api-tools\ec2-api-tools-1.3-62308\b
```

Now run the ec2-describe-regions command, it should return the current list of regions that are available:

```
C:\AWS> ec2-describe-regions
```

```
C:\Windows\system32\cmd.exe

c:\AWS>ec2-describe-regions
REGION  eu-west-1       ec2.eu-west-1.amazonaws.com
REGION  us-east-1       ec2.us-east-1.amazonaws.com
REGION  ap-northeast-1  ec2.ap-northeast-1.amazonaws.com
REGION  us-west-1       ec2.us-west-1.amazonaws.com
REGION  ap-southeast-1  ec2.ap-southeast-1.amazonaws.com

c:\AWS>
```

If the result returned from the command is similar to the one mentioned earlier, then the AWS command-line tools have been installed successfully!

Starting an EC2 instance

Now that we have installed the AWS command-line tools, it's time to start an EC2 instance from the command line. To start an instance, you will need to firstly find out its **AMI ID**. Run the following command to get a list of all of the AMIs owned by you:

```
C:\AWS> ec2-describe-images -o self
```

The AMI ID is the second column where the values start with **ami-**. Once you have selected the AMI you are going to use as a base for your EC2 instance, you can start it with the following command:

```
C:\AWS> ec2-run-instances ami-70b24319 -g migrate_to_aws_secure -k
migrate_to_aws_key_pair --availability-zone us-east-1a --instance-type
t1.micro --monitor
```

Where:

- -g <The security group>
- -k <The key pair>
- --availability-zone <Where you would like your instance to start>
- --monitor <turn on monitoring for this instance>
- --instance-type <the type of instance you want to launch for example t1.micro>

After your instance has started, the **Instance ID** will be returned at the screen prompt. You can use this Instance ID to label your instance using the following command:

```
C:\AWS> ec2-create-tags i-cc9b92a1 --tag "Name=DB01"
```

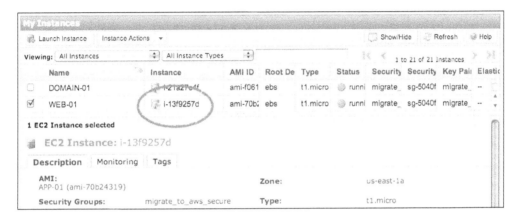

You should be able to see your instance running in the AWS Console, if it hasn't appeared, try clicking on the **Refresh** button:

Stopping an EC2 instance

1. To stop an instance you will need to know its Instance ID. To get a list of running instances execute the following command:

   ```
   C:\AWS> ec2-describe-instances --filter "instance-state-
   name=running"
   ```

2. The Instance ID is the second column starting with an "**i-**". After you have determined the Instance ID, then use the following command to terminate it:

   ```
   C:\AWS> ec2-terminate-instances i-cc9b92a1
   ```

3. To stop an instance instead of terminating it, use the following command:

   ```
   C:\AWS> ec2-stop-instances i-cc9b92a1
   ```

4. For a full list of the AWS EC2 commands, go to http://docs.
   amazonwebservices.com/AWSEC2/latest/CommandLineReference/
   command-reference.html.

Summary

In this chapter, we have learned how to create an account on AWS EC2 and start EC2 instances. We have created bundled AMI images from existing instances and used them as the base for starting new EC2 instances. We have also learned how to install the EC2 command-line tools and use them to manage EC2.

In the next chapter, we will be looking at how storage works on Amazon, including Elastic Block Store (EBS) volumes and Simple Storage Service (S3) volumes.

4
How Storage Works on Amazon

In this chapter, we will look at how Amazon manages storage. We will look at the differences between S3 and EBS storage and how to implement both. We will create the storage locations that we will need for our sample application and look at how to implement storage using both the AWS console and the AWS command line.

Getting started with S3

In *Chapter 3, Getting Started with AWS and Amazon EC2*, we briefly covered creating an S3 bucket, and in *Chapter 2, Mapping your Enterprise Requirements Against Amazon's Offerings*, we briefly looked at the S3 service as a whole. We covered the basics for S3 and also looked at how S3 is accessed. Most importantly, we learned that S3 is not a traditional filesystem like our C:\ drive.

Creating a S3 bucket with logging

Logging provides detailed information on who accessed what data in your bucket and when. However, to turn on logging for a bucket, an existing bucket must have already been created to hold the logging information, as this is where AWS stores it.

To create a bucket with logging, click on the **Create Bucket** button in the **Buckets** sidebar as in *Chapter 3, Getting Started with AWS and Amazon EC2*:

This time, however, click on the **Set Up Logging** button. You will be presented with a dialog that allows you to choose the location for the logging information, as well as the prefix for your logging data:

You will note that we have pointed the logging information back at the original bucket **migrate_to_aws_01** that we created in *Chapter 3, Getting Started with AWS and Amazon EC2*.

Logging information will not appear immediately; however, a file will be created every few minutes depending on activity. The following screenshot shows an example of the files that are created:

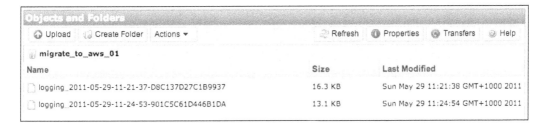

 Before jumping right into the command-line tools, it should be noted that the AWS Console includes a Java-based multi-file upload utility that allows a maximum size of 300 MB for each file.

Using the S3 command-line tools

Unfortunately, Amazon does not provide official command-line tools for S3 similar to the tools they have provided for EC2. However, there is an excellent simple free utility provided at `http://s3.codeplex.com`, called `S3.exe`, that requires no installation and runs without the requirement of third-party packages.

To install the program, just download it from the website and copy it to your **C:\AWS** folder.

Setting up your credentials with S3.exe

Before we can run `S3.exe`, we first need to set up our credentials. To do that you will need to get your **S3 Access Key** and your **S3 Secret Access Key** from the credentials page of your AWS account. Browse to the following location in your browser, `https://aws-portal.amazon.com/gp/aws/developer/account/index.html?ie=UTF8&action=access-key` and scroll down to the **Access Credentials** section:

The Access Key is displayed in this screen; however, to get your Secret Access Key you will need to click on the **Show** link under the **Secret Access Key** heading.

Run the following command to set up s3.exe:

```
C:\AWS>s3 auth AKIAIIJXIP5XC6NW3KTQ
   9UpktBlqDroY5C4Q7OnlF1pNXtK332TslYFsWy9R
```

To check that the tool has been installed correctly, run the s3 list command:

```
C:\AWS>s3 list
```

You should get the following result:

Copying files to S3 using S3.exe

First, create a file called **myfile.txt** in the **C:\AWS** directory.

To copy this file to an S3 bucket that you own, use the following command:

c:\AWS>s3 put migrate_to_aws_02 myfile.txt

```
C:\Windows\system32\cmd.exe

c:\AWS>s3 put migrate_to_aws_02 myfile.txt
s3.exe version 1.7 - check for updates at http://s3.codeplex.com

Please enter your encryption password: ......
myfile.txt

c:\AWS>
```

This command copies the file to the **migrate_to_aws_02** bucket with the default permissions of full control for the owner.

 You will need to refresh the AWS Console to see the file listed.

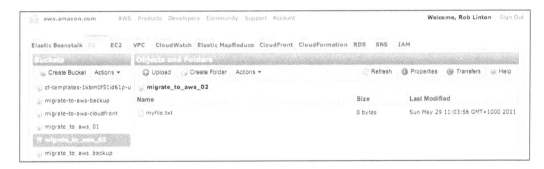

Uploading larger files to AWS can be problematic, as any network connectivity issues during the upload will terminate the upload. To upload larger files, use the following syntax:

C:\AWS>s3 put migrate_to_aws_02/mybigfile/ mybigfile.txt /big

```
C:\Windows\system32\cmd.exe

c:\AWS>s3 put migrate_to_aws_02/mybigfile/ mybigfile.txt /big
s3.exe version 1.7 - check for updates at http://s3.codeplex.com

Please enter your encryption password: ......
mybigfile/mybigfile.txt.000
mybigfile/mybigfile.txt.001

c:\AWS>
```

This breaks the upload into small chunks, which can be reversed when getting the file back again.

 If you run the same command again, you will note that no chunks are uploaded. This is because S3.exe does not upload a chunk again if the checksum matches.

Retrieving files from S3 using S3.exe

Retrieving files from S3 is the reverse of copying files up to S3.

To get a single file back use:

C:\AWS>s3 get migrate_to_aws_02/myfile.txt

To get our big file back again use:

C:\AWS>s3 get migrate_to_aws_02/mybigfile/mybigfile.txt /big

```
C:\Windows\system32\cmd.exe

c:\AWS>s3 get migrate_to_aws_02/mybigfile/mybigfile.txt /big
s3.exe version 1.7 - check for updates at http://s3.codeplex.com

Please enter your encryption password: ......
migrate_to_aws_02/mybigfile/mybigfile.txt.000
migrate_to_aws_02/mybigfile/mybigfile.txt.001

c:\AWS>
```

 The S3.exe command automatically recombines our large file chunks back into a single file.

Importing and exporting large amounts of data in and out of S3

Because S3 lives in the cloud within Amazon's data centers, it may be costly and time consuming to transfer large amounts of data to and from Amazon's data center to your own data center. An example of a large file transfer may be a large database backup file that you may wish to migrate from your own data center to AWS.

Luckily for us, Amazon provides the AWS Import/Export Service for the US Standard and EU (Ireland) regions. However, this service is not supported for the other two regions at this time.

The AWS Import service allows you to place your data on a portable hard drive and physically mail your hard disk to Amazon for uploading/downloading of your data from within Amazon's data center.

Amazon provides the following recommendations for when to use this service.

- If your connection is 1.55Mbps and your data is 100GB or more
- If your connection is 10Mbps and your data is 600GB or more
- If your connection is 44.736Mbps and your data is 2TB or more
- If your connection is 100Mbps and your data is 5TB or more

 Make sure if you choose either the US West (California) or Asia Pacific (Singapore) regions that you do not need access to the AWS Import/Export service, as it is not available in these regions.

Setting up the Import/Export service

To begin using this service once again, you will need to sign up for this service separately from your other services. Click on the **Sign Up for AWS Import/Export** button located on the product page http://aws.amazon.com/importexport, confirm the pricing and click on the **Complete Sign Up** button.

Once again, you will need to wait for the service to become active:

Activating Subscription...

We are in the process of activating your subscription so that you can begin using this service. We will email you when your subscription becomes active so that you can begin using AWS Import/Export. For most customers, this process usually only take a couple minutes (but can sometimes take a few hours if additional account verification is required).

You will get an email at   once your subscription to AWS Import/Export is complete. You will then be able to begin using this service.

Thank you for your patience.

Current costs are:

Cost Type	US East	US West	EU	APAC
Device handling	$80	$80	$80	$99
Data loading time	$2.49 per data loading hour	$2.49 per data loading hour	$2.49 per data loading hour	$2.99 per data loading hour

Using the Import/Export service

To use the Import/Export service, first make sure that your external disk device conforms to Amazon's specifications.

Confirming your device specifications

The details are specified at `http://aws.amazon.com/importexport/#supported_devices`, but essentially as long as it is a standard external USB 2.0 hard drive or a rack mountable device less than 8Us supporting eSATA then you will have no problems.

 Remember to supply a US power plug adapter if you are not located in the United States.

Downloading and installing the command-line service tool

Once you have confirmed that your device meets Amazon's specifications, download the command-line tools for the Import/Export service. At this time, it is not possible to use this service from the AWS Console. The tools are located at `http://awsimportexport.s3.amazonaws.com/importexport-webservice-tool.zip`.

Copy the `.zip` file to the `C:\AWS` directory and unzip them, they will most likely end up in the following directory, **C:\AWS\importexport-webservice-tool**.

Creating a job

1. To create a job, change directory to the **C:\AWS\importexport-webservice-tool** directory, open notepad, and paste the following text into a new file:

```
manifestVersion: 2.0
bucket: migrate_to_aws_01
accessKeyId: AKIAIIJXIP5XC6NW3KTQ
deviceId: 12345678
eraseDevice: no
returnAddress:
  name: Rob Linton
```

```
      street1: Level 1, Migrate St
      city: Amazon City
      stateOrProvince: Amazon
      postalCode: 1000
      phoneNumber: 12345678
      country: Amazonia
   customs:
      dataDescription: Test Data
      encryptedData: yes
      encryptionClassification: 5D992
      exportCertifierName: Rob Linton
      requiresExportLicense: no
      deviceValue: 250.00
      deviceCountryOfOrigin: China
      deviceType: externalStorageDevice
```

2. Edit the text to reflect your own postal address, **accessKeyId**, bucket name, and save the file as `MyManifest.txt`. For more information on the customs configuration items refer to `http://docs.amazonwebservices.com/AWSImportExport/latest/DG/index.html?ManifestFileRef_international.html`.

 If you are located outside of the United States a customs section in the manifest is a requirement.

3. In the same folder open the `AWSCredentials.properties` file in notepad, and copy and paste in both your AWS Access Key ID and your AWS Secret Access Key. The file should look like this:

 # Fill in your AWS Access Key ID and Secret Access Key

 # http://aws.amazon.com/security-credentials

accessKeyId:AKIAIIJXIP5XC6NW3KTQ

secretKey:9UpktBlqDroY5C4Q7OnlF1pNXtK332TslYFsWy9R

4. Now that you have created the required files, run the following command in the same directory.

```
C:\AWS\importexport-webservice-tool>java -jar
   lib/AWSImportExportWebServiceTool-1.0.jar CreateJob Import
   MyManifest.txt .
```

If you have been following this book step by step, you will have already installed Java in *Chapter 3, Getting Started with AWS and Amazon EC2*.

```
C:\Windows\system32\cmd.exe

c:\AWS\importexport-webservice-tool>java -jar lib/AWSImportExportWebServiceTool-1.0.jar CreateJob Import MyManifest.txt .
SIGNATURE file already found at c:\AWS\importexport-webservice-tool\.\SIGNATURE
Overwrite existing SIGNATURE file? <Yes/No> > yes
............
JOB CREATED

JobId:   TTURP
JobType: Import
**************************************
* AwsShippingAddress                 *
**************************************
AWS Import/Export
JOBID TTURP
2646 Rainier Ave South Suite 1060
Seattle, WA 98144
**************************************
* SignatureFileContents              *
**************************************
version:2.0
signingMethod:HmacSHA1
jobid:TTURP
signature:XoiwLzHmfa8ghQCpwtOxnPtzYKg=


Writing SignatureFileContents to c:\AWS\importexport-webservice-tool\.\SIGNATURE

c:\AWS\importexport-webservice-tool>
```

Your job will be created along with a `.SIGNATURE` file in the same directory.

Copying the data to your disk device

Now you are ready to copy your data to your external disk device. However, before you start, it is mandatory to copy the `.SIGNATURE` file created in the previous step into the root directory of your disk device.

Sending your disk device

Once your data and the `.SIGNATURE` file have been copied to your disk device, print out the packing slip and fill out the details. The **JOBID** can be obtained in the output from your earlier create job request, in our example the **JOBID** is **XHNHC**. The **DEVICE IDENTIFIER** is the device serial number, which was entered into the manifest file, in our example it was **12345678**.

The following is a representation of the packing slip image:

amazon web services~ *AWS Import/Export*

PACKING SLIP

INSTRUCTIONS
1. Complete this packing slip with date, AWS account e-mail, JOBID, and Device Identifier.
2. Place this packing slip inside the box with your media.
3. Send the box to the AWS Address specified in the CREATE JOB response e-mail.

DATE	AWS ACCOUNT EMAIL
CONTACT	PHONE NUMBER/E-MAIL ADDRESS
JOBID	DEVICE IDENTIFIER/SERIAL NUMBER

The packing slip must be enclosed in the package used to send your disk device.

Each package can have only one storage device and one packing slip, multiple storage devices must be sent separately.

Address the package with the address output in the create job request:

AWS Import/Export

JOBID TTVRP

2646 Rainier Ave South Suite 1060

Seattle, WA 98144

 Please note that this address may change depending on what region you are sending your data to. The correct address will always be returned from the Create Job command in the AWS Import/Export Tool.

Managing your Import/Export jobs

Once your job has been submitted, the only way to get the current status of your job or to modify your job is to run the AWS Import/Export command-line tool. Here is an example of how to list your jobs and how to cancel a job.

To get a list of your current jobs, you can run the following command:

```
C:\AWS\importexport-webservice-tool>java -jar
  lib/AWSImportExportWebServiceTool-1.0.jar ListJobs
```

To cancel a job, you can run the following command:

```
C:\AWS\importexport-webservice-tool>java -jar
   lib/AWSImportExportWebServiceTool-1.0.jar CancelJob XHNHC
```

Accessing S3 using third-party tools

When S3 was first introduced, initially the access to it was via the S3 API.

Since then however, there have been a number of tools developed to facilitate accessing objects stored in S3. One of the most recent is the AWS console. Another tool is **S3Fox** (http://www.s3fox.net), a plugin for the Firefox browser. However, both of these tools are web-based interfaces to S3, and not integrated into Windows itself.

Commercial products to look at if you would like to create a virtual filesystem under Windows are:

- Galdinet (http://www.gladinet.com)
- Jungledisk (http://www.jungledisk.com)
- CloudBerry (http://www.cloudberry.com)

Getting started with EBS

Elastic Block Store (EBS) provides EC2 instances access to persistent disk in a filesystem. EBS is fast (much faster than S3), and does not have the same limitations surrounding access and naming that S3 has.

Creating an EBS volume

1. To create an EBS volume click on the EC2 tab in the AWS console, click on the **Volumes** link in the **Navigation** section, and then click on the **Create Volume** button.

2. The first thing you will notice in the **Create Volume** dialog is that you must select an **Availability Zone**. This is because EBS volumes are locked to a particular availability zone and cannot be accessed in any other zone from an EC2 instance.

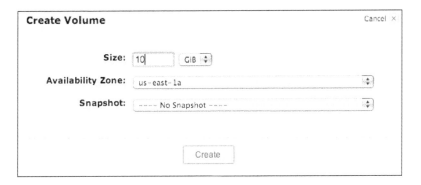

3. Leave the Snapshot field blank for the moment and click on create.

4. The Volume will appear with a status of **creating** in the status window:

5. When it is available, its status will change to **available**. Before we go any further, make sure you have at least one EC2 instance running so that we can attach the new volume to running in the same availability zone.

6. Right-click on the AWS Volume and select **Attach Volume**:

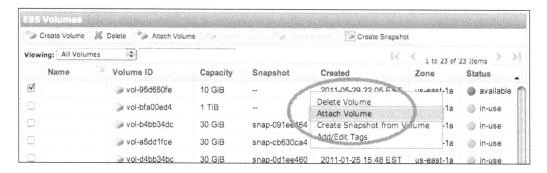

7. Once you have selected **Attach Volume**, the following dialog will appear:

8. You can see straightaway that the Instance does not show the **Tag Name**, but instead only shows the **Instance Id**. So before you go ahead and attach this volume, make sure that you write down the instance ID of the instance that you would like to attach this volume to.

9. The Device field is the Windows device name that the volume will be attached to. Note that the dialog states that the allowable devices are devices xvdf through to xvdp, attaching any devices out of this range will result in the volume not attaching successfully.

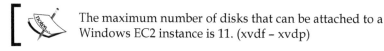

   The maximum number of disks that can be attached to a Windows EC2 instance is 11. (xvdf – xvdp)

10. After you have selected **Attach**, it will take a moment for the disk to become active on the selected instance.

It is important to note that a given EBS volume can only be attached to one single EC2 instance at a time; however, a single EC2 instance can have multiple EBS volumes attached to it.

11. The first time the disk is attached to an instance, you may find that the disk is **Offline** in disk manager; you will need to bring the disk online and initialize it, prior to creating a partition and formatting it:

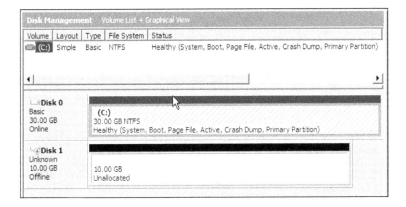

12. When assigning a drive letter it is best to be consistent, I like to assign the same drive letter as the device name, for example, F : \ for the xvdf device. Note that I have named the drive label to **F-DRIVE** in this case:

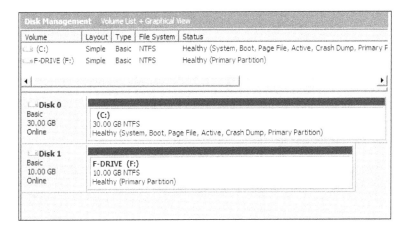

13. To ensure that the same drive mapping occurs next time the disk is mounted, update the disk mapping in the **EC2 Service Properties**.

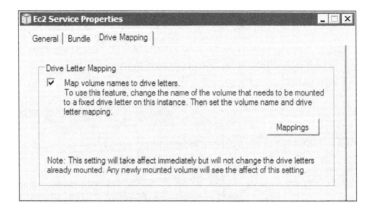

14. Click on the **Mappings** button and create entries for the disks that you will be attaching.

15. This is an example of the drive mappings we will be using for our sample application:

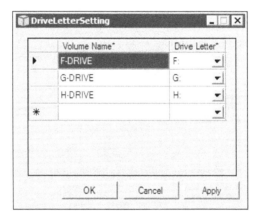

Note that the Volume Names have been set to match the names that were set in the disk manager.

 By setting the Drive Letter Mappings in the EC2 Service Properties, we can ensure that volumes will always be mapped to the same drive letters.

Creating an EBS snapshot

Once we have attached an EBS volume to our running EC2 instance, the drive can be accessed just like any other hard drive or SAN volume. Now that the F drive has been attached in our example, we are going to edit some data and create a snapshot, which can be attached to another instance in a different availability zone.

1. To create a snapshot, first create a text file in **F:\myfile.txt** and edit it with the value **Snapshot One**:

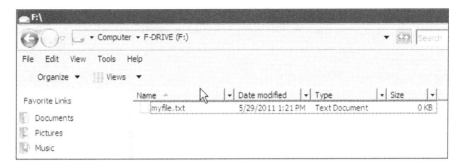

2. We will use this file to demonstrate the snapshot process.

3. Now right-click on the Volume in the AWS Console and select Create Snapshot from the pop-up menu as shown in the next screenshot.

 Windows volumes have a disk cache, which is kept in memory, so if a snapshot is taken while the Windows server is still running, the data on the disk may not be consistent. If possible, do not take a snapshot of an EBS volume on a Windows server unless the server is in a stopped state.

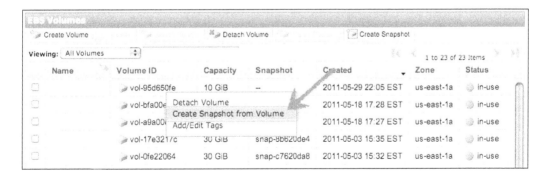

4. The dialog that pops up will require you to give the snapshot a name, in this case, we have named our snapshot **Snapshot One**:

5. The snapshot will then be queued. To see all of the current snapshots click on the **Snapshots** link in the **Navigator** pane in the AWS Console:

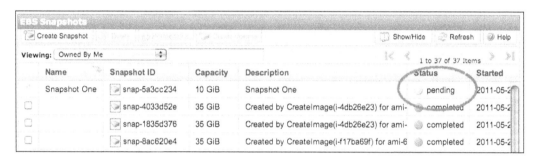

 Please note, AWS uses snapshots to keep track of your AMI bundles, so you will see more snapshots in this list than just the ones created by you.

6. Now that we have a snapshot, (Snapshot One), right-click on the snapshot and select **Create Volume from Snapshot** in the pop-up menu:

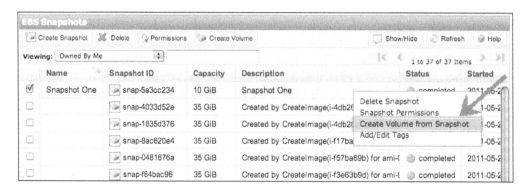

7. When creating the volume you will have the option of selecting a different availability zone:

8. This time select the **us-east-1b** availability zone and click on create. The new volume will be created in the new availability zone and will be an exact copy of the original volume at the time the snapshot was initiated:

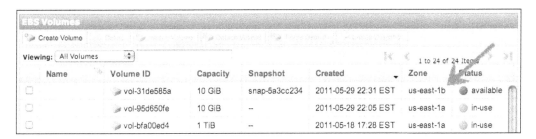

9. When the volume has finished creating, attempt to attach it to the original instance that it was created from. You will note that this is not possible as the new volume is now in a different availability zone to the original volume.

To migrate volumes between availability zones, create a snapshot from the volume in the source availability zone, and re-create the volume from the snapshot in the new availability zone.

10. Start an instance in the same availability zone as our new volume and attach it.

The first time the volume is attached to an instance after being created from a snapshot, the volume will need to be set Online in disk manager.

An important note about EBS

EBS volumes do not lose their data when they are detached from an EC2 instance. The data still persists on the EBS volume. It is only when the EBS volume is deleted that the data is destroyed. Please make sure to create a snapshot of the volume before a volume is deleted, that way if you accidentally delete the wrong volume, you can recover by recreating the volume from the snapshot.

Using the EBS command-line tools

EBS volumes can be managed with the EC2 command-line tools.

- To create an EBS volume, run the following command:

```
C:\AWS> ec2-create-volume  --size 20 --availability-zone us-east-
1a
```

This creates a volume 20Gb in size in the **us-east-1a** availability zone and returns the **Volume Id**.

To attach a volume to an instance, run the following command:

```
C:\AWS> ec2-attach-volume vol-59da5c32  -i i-b73186db -d xvdf
```

This attaches volume **vol-59da5c32** to instance **i-b73186db** on device **xvdf**.

To detach the volume, run the following command:

```
C:\AWS>ec2-detach-volume vol-59da5c32
```

Finally, to delete the volume, run the following command:

```
C:\AWS>ec2-delete-volume vol-59da5c32
```

```
C:\Windows\system32\cmd.exe

c:\AWS>ec2-create-volume  --size 20 --availability-zone us-east-1a
VOLUME  vol-59da5c32   20              us-east-1a      creating        2011-05-29T12:44:19+0000
c:\AWS>ec2-attach-volume vol-59da5c32 -i i-b73186db -d xvdf
ATTACHMENT       vol-59da5c32    i-b73186db      xvdf    attaching       2011-05-29T12:44:54+0000
c:\AWS>ec2-detach-volume vol-59da5c32
ATTACHMENT       vol-59da5c32    i-b73186db      xvdf    detaching       2011-05-29T12:45:01+0000
c:\AWS>ec2-delete-volume vol-59da5c32
VOLUME  vol-59da5c32
c:\AWS>_
```

Setting up storage for our sample application

Now that we have covered S3 and EBS in detail, it's time to use these services to create storage for our sample application. In our sample application, we have two web servers, two application servers, two database servers, and one domain controller.

Group	Volumes	
Web Servers	Data – 10Gb	For our web servers, we will be creating a small EBS volume of 10Gb in size for each web server. We will use this volume to store the actual website data, which will be linked to IIS via a virtual directory.
Application Servers	Data – 10Gb	For our application servers, we will be creating a small EBS volume of 10Gb in size.
Database Servers	Data – 200Gb	For our database servers, we will be creating three volumes for each server.
	Log – 200Gb	
	Backup – 200Gb	
Domain Controller	Data – 10Gb	For our domain controller server, we will be creating a small EBS volume of 10Gb in size.

Backup storage on S3

Along with the previous EBS storage, we will be creating a shared backup storage bucket on S3. The name for this storage location will be **migrate_to_aws_backup**. Our database backups will be copied to this location.

Summary

In this chapter, we learned about storage in detail in AWS. We learned about the differences between EBS and S3 and how to create and manage storage on both of these services. We also covered how to import large amounts of data into S3 and created the storage volumes we will need for our sample enterprise application.

In the next chapter, we will learn how Amazon approaches networking, load balancing and VPNs. We will also set up the networking and firewall requirements for our sample application.

5
Amazon's Approach to Networking

In this chapter, we will cover Elastic IPs, Elastic Load Balancing, Virtual Private Clouds, and CloudFront. We'll step through the architecture, setup, and configuration details that are relevant to the enterprise.

Once we have looked at how AWS does networking, we will configure our sample application to use Amazon's approach.

An overview of AWS networking

For those of you who are familiar with general networking principles, AWS will be a substantially different beast from what you are used to. Within an enterprise you will be familiar with IP subnets and routing between those subnets. Perhaps each floor of your office has a different subnet, or perhaps each switch in your data center has its own **Virtual Lan** (**VLAN**), but whatever your current setup is, it will most likely look something like the following:

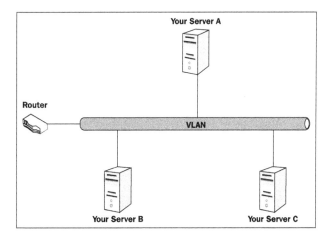

Each server is clearly on its own subnet, segregated into VLANs and routed by dedicated routers.

However, within AWS, networking looks substantially different.

Firstly, IP addresses are allocated automatically and change every time a server is restarted. Servers on AWS exist in a pool of servers, which can be located on any subnet within that availability region. Routing is managed by Amazon, and it is possible that there may be 1+n routers between all of the servers within your application:

 This is different for an Amazon VPC setup, as we will see later on in this chapter.

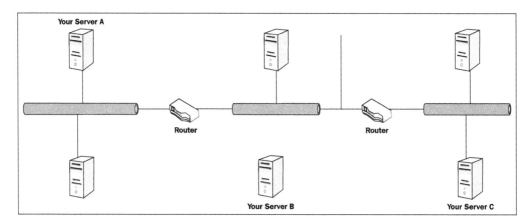

To give an example of this, let's start three EC2 instances in the same availability zone and compare their IP addresses.

The IP addresses allocated to each of these instances were:

- 10.125.2.118
- 10.220.107.120
- 10.220.106.24

Doing a **tracert** between the instances showed three hops between two of the machines:

```
Administrator: Command Prompt

C:\Users\Administrator>tracert 10.220.106.24

Tracing route to domU-12-31-38-04-69-EA.compute-1.internal [10.220.106.24]
over a maximum of 30 hops:

  1    <1 ms    <1 ms    <1 ms  ip-10-125-0-2.ec2.internal [10.125.0.2]
  2    <1 ms    <1 ms    <1 ms  216.182.232.100
  3    <1 ms    <1 ms    <1 ms  216.182.232.163
  4     2 ms    <1 ms    <1 ms  domU-12-31-38-04-69-EA.compute-1.internal [10.220.106.24]

Trace complete.
```

Examining internal versus external IP addresses

One thing you will notice about all of your instances is that they appear to have two IP addresses even though your EC2 instance has only one physical adapter!

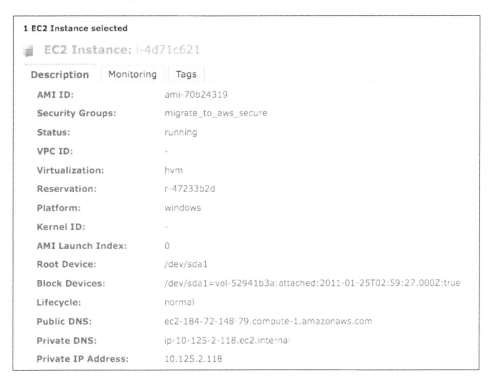

1 EC2 Instance selected	
EC2 Instance: i-4d71c621	
Description Monitoring Tags	
AMI ID:	ami-70b24319
Security Groups:	migrate_to_aws_secure
Status:	running
VPC ID:	-
Virtualization:	hvm
Reservation:	r-47233b2d
Platform:	windows
Kernel ID:	-
AMI Launch Index:	0
Root Device:	/dev/sda1
Block Devices:	/dev/sda1=vol-52941b3a:attached:2011-01-25T02:59:27.000Z:true
Lifecycle:	normal
Public DNS:	ec2-184-72-148-79.compute-1.amazonaws.com
Private DNS:	ip-10-125-2-118.ec2.internal
Private IP Address:	10.125.2.118

1. To test this, start up an instance; log in to the **EC2 Instance** and start up a Cmd Prompt.

2. Firstly, ping the **Private DNS**, the IP address that is returned should be the same as the **Private IP Address (10.125.2.118)** listed in your Instance properties.

3. Now ping the **Public DNS**, the IP address returned is the same as the **Private DNS**! This is because all DNS lookups from within the AWS infrastructure always return the Private IP address, not the Public IP address.

4. Now start up a Cmd Prompt on your own local computer and repeat the ping to the Public Address of your EC2 instance. This time you will see the external IP address of your EC2 instance, don't worry if you receive the following response:

```
> PING ec2-184-72-148-79.compute-1.amazonaws.com (184.72.148.79):
56 data bytes
> Request timeout for icmp_seq 0
```

It's enough for now to see that the IP address is 184.72.148.79, different from our internal IP address.

> It is important to differentiate between the external and internal IP address when referencing EC2 instances, as this can have a major impact on the security groups used to access these instances, which we will see later on.

Allocating elastic IPs

Right now you may be asking how is it possible to design an application stack on AWS if both the DNS and IP address change dynamically, and in addition it is likely that your EC2 instances will not exist on the same subnet.

We have briefly touched on Elastic IP addresses in *Chapter 2, Mapping your Enterprise Requirements Against Amazon's Offerings*. Let's discuss them further now.

Amazon allocates Elastic IP addresses automatically on request. Elastic IPs do not designate a particular subnet, nor do they exist on the same subnet (except by sheer coincidence). However, once an Elastic IP has been allocated to a particular EC2 instance, the IP address of that instance will remain fixed for the lifetime of that instance. This includes stopping and restarting the instance.

> Terminating an EC2 instance will release the Elastic IP address associated with it.

Associating an Elastic IP address with an EC2 instance will replace the existing External IP address of that instance, as well as replacing the External DNS of that instance.

Remember that while elastic IP addresses are free, you will be charged if they have been allocated but not used.

Here is an example of an EC2 instance prior to having an Elastic IP associated:

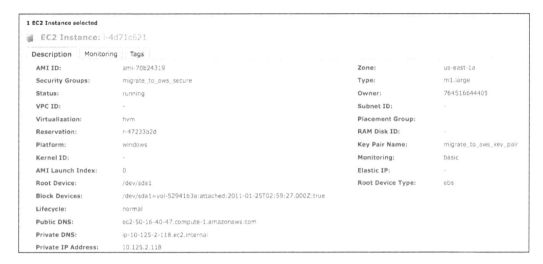

After allocating an Elastic IP address of **184.73.175.58** and associating it with this instance, it now looks like:

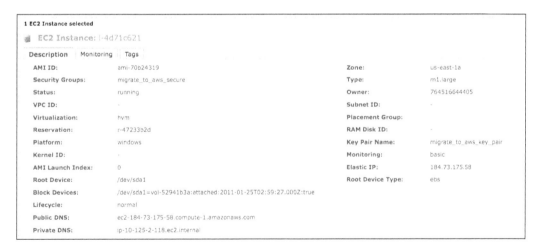

Notice that the **Public DNS** name has changed and that there is now a value in the **Elastic IP** field.

 Note that the Public DNS of an EC2 instance also changes when associating an Elastic IP with an instance.

Security groups and internal versus external IP addresses

We covered security groups briefly in *Chapter 2, Mapping your Enterprise Requirements Against Amazon's Offerings* but let's look at how they impact communication between EC2 instances when using Elastic IP addresses.

When setting up security groups within AWS, it is possible to not only specify source IP addresses, but also to specify another security group as the source. Using this functionality it is possible to allocate groups of servers to specific security groups, such as 'web servers' or 'app servers', and then reference the security group rather than an IP address as the source.

Here is an example of the **Web Servers** security group:

As you can see **Port 80** is allowed from anywhere, as is RDP. (Usually, RDP would be restricted to the external IP address of your enterprise's firewall).

The following screenshot is an example of the **App Servers** security group:

As you can see, we have allowed all communication from the Web Servers to the App Servers.

If we log on to a Web Server and attempt to ping the Private IP address *or* the Public IP address on one of the app servers, then we should get the following result:

Pinging the Public IP address will resolve to the
Private IP address when accessed from inside the
AWS infrastructure.

However, what happens if we ping the Public IP address directly?

```
Administrator: C:\Windows\system32\cmd.exe
C:\Users\Administrator>ping ec2-50-16-142-110.compute-1.amazonaws.com

Pinging ec2-50-16-142-110.compute-1.amazonaws.com [10.122.114.138] with 32 bytes of data:
Reply from 10.122.114.138: bytes=32 time=16ms TTL=128
Reply from 10.122.114.138: bytes=32 time<1ms TTL=128
Reply from 10.122.114.138: bytes=32 time<1ms TTL=128
Reply from 10.122.114.138: bytes=32 time<1ms TTL=128

Ping statistics for 10.122.114.138:
    Packets: Sent = 4, Received = 4, Lost = 0 (0% loss),
Approximate round trip times in milli-seconds:
    Minimum = 0ms, Maximum = 16ms, Average = 4ms

C:\Users\Administrator>ping 50.16.142.110

Pinging 50.16.142.110 with 32 bytes of data:
Request timed out.
Request timed out.
Request timed out.
Request timed out.

Ping statistics for 50.16.142.110:
    Packets: Sent = 4, Received = 0, Lost = 4 (100% loss),
```

The access is blocked! The reason being, AWS security groups always reference
the Private IP address when resolving source security groups. In this case, the
App Servers allow communication from the Web Servers, but only on their
Private IP address.

Security groups allow access from AWS Private
IP address only.

However, we still don't have a static IP address on our App Servers, and without
one the web servers won't know where to send their requests. So let's go ahead and
add an Elastic IP address to each of the App Servers and see how that changes our
security groups.

You will need to wait a few minutes for the
DNS change to take effect.

But, hang on a minute! We have allocated an Elastic IP address, which gets associated with the Public or external DNS. But doesn't this map to the internal IP address anyway?

Let's try it!

```
Administrator: C:\Windows\system32\cmd.exe

C:\Users\Administrator>ping ec2-184-73-175-58.compute-1.amazonaws.com

Pinging ec2-184-73-175-58.compute-1.amazonaws.com [10.122.114.138] with 32 bytes of data:
Reply from 10.122.114.138: bytes=32 time=15ms TTL=128
Reply from 10.122.114.138: bytes=32 time<1ms TTL=128
Reply from 10.122.114.138: bytes=32 time<1ms TTL=128
Reply from 10.122.114.138: bytes=32 time<1ms TTL=128

Ping statistics for 10.122.114.138:
    Packets: Sent = 4, Received = 4, Lost = 0 (0% loss),
Approximate round trip times in milli-seconds:
    Minimum = 0ms, Maximum = 15ms, Average = 3ms

C:\Users\Administrator>_
```

Pinging the Public DNS once again resolves to the Private IP. This is the intentional behavior for AWS. By design, allocating an Elastic IP forces the Public DNS to be permanently fixed for the life of that instance. However, it is the Private IP, which is actually used to access the App Server and referenced when checked against the valid security groups.

 When an Elastic IP address has been allocated, always reference the Public DNS from within AWS to ensure that you are connecting to the correct internal IP address, never reference the internal IP address directly.

Handling domain controllers in AWS

The above is true for just about all communications within AWS except for the following:

Domain controllers in AWS are handled somewhat differently.

Computers (or EC2 instances), which are part of a domain, must have their DNS entry set to point to their domain controller. Since IP addresses can change in AWS, it is a requirement to assign an elastic IP address to the domain controller to ensure that it does not change.

The problem with this is that, by definition, elastic IP addresses are external-facing and represent the public IP address of the domain controller, they do not replace the internally allocated IP address on the domain controller.

Remember that security groups only manage security between internal IP addresses, this means that any security groups allowing access between servers that are part of the domain and the domain controller are now irrelevant.

The workaround for this is to allocate an Elastic IP address to all servers accessing a DC within AWS and to manually add each of the Public Elastic IP addresses to the security group on the DC individually.

 Setting up our sample application database layer is explained step-by-step later on in this chapter.

Amazon VPC

We gave an overview of Amazon VPC in *Chapter 1, Understanding Amazon Web Services* and *Chapter 2, Mapping your Enterprise Requirements Against Amazon's Offerings*, so we already know that Amazon VPC gives us a sandbox, which is completely isolated from the general Interenet and is only available from our own enterprise corporate network. In this section, you will learn how to create a VPC and start up an EC2 instance in that VPC.

Creating the AWS VPC

A VPC is a private part of the Amazon cloud that is only accessible to your own organization. The following are the steps to create your own VPC:

1. To create the AWS VPC, select the **VPC** tab in the AWS console.

2. If you have yet to create a VPC, it will look like the following screenshot:

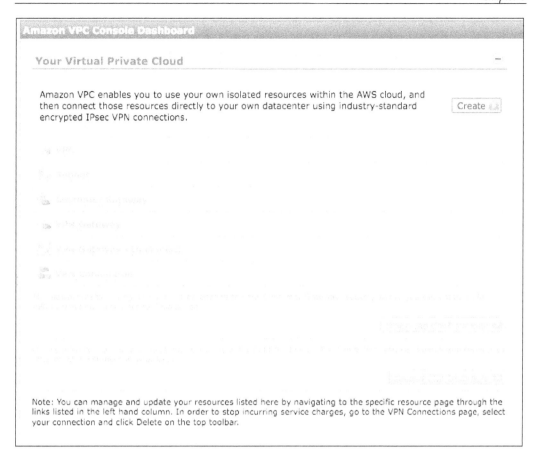

3. To begin the process click on the **Create** button. You will be prompted with the following dialog:

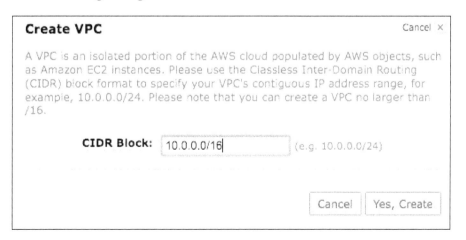

A **CIDR Block** is a compact way of specifying a contiguous range of IP addresses. CIDR replaces the classful method of specifying IP address ranges where the range was specified by an IP address and a bitmask. Here are some examples:

CIDR	Classful Network	IP address range
10.0.0.1/32	10.0.0.1/255.255.255.255	10.0.0.1 – 10.0.0.1
10.0.0.0/24	10.0.0.0/255.255.255.0	10.0.0.0 – 10.0.0.255
10.0.0.0/16	10.0.0.0/255.255.0.0	10.0.0.0 – 10.0.255.255

4. This essentially is asking for the subnet range for all of the EC2 instances that will reside in your VPC. The example shown (**10.0.0.0/16**) will allow you to create 65536 EC2 instances.

 Actually the number is slightly less as AWS reserves the first 4 IP address in each range for its own use.

AWS allows you to create up to a class B range:

255.255.0.0   **11111111.11111111.00000000.00000000 /16**   **class B**

 It is recommended that you over-allocate as many as you think you will ultimately need, as it is not possible to alter this in the future without dismantling the VPN and terminating all of the EC2 instances that are currently running inside it.

5. So unless there is an issue with overlapping IP address ranges, allocate the maximum:

CIDR Block: 10.0.0.0/16

6. Next you will need to create at least one subnet. Be sure to create the subnet large enough for what you will need, as it is not possible to resize it once it has been created.

7. Here you can see an example of the subnets that I have created.

 Subnets are used in networking to separate group servers and network traffic. Typically broadcasting traffic is restricted to the local subnet and all servers in the same network are directly visible to all other servers in the same subnet. Subnets are used to ensure that IP address is allocated efficiently or to enhance routing efficiency. Firewalls often base rules on source subnets rather than individual IP addresses.

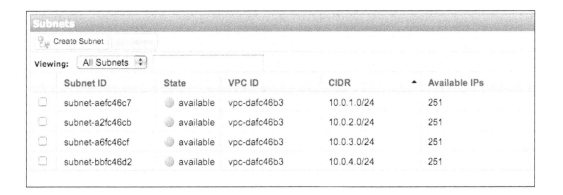

 Note that each subnet only has 251 IP addresses available, as the first four are reserved by AWS.

8. Once you have created your subnets you can go ahead and create a **Customer Gateway**. This is your side of the VPN and the only information that you will need for this is the external IP address of the firewall in your enterprise that will be handling the VPN connection.

9. Once this is created, go ahead and click on the **Create** button for the **VPN Gateway**, this is the AWS side of the VPN connection.

10. After creating the AWS side of the VPN, you will now need to attach this to your VPC. (At this time, AWS limits you to one VPC anyway, so this step is a one-click action).

11. Finally, you will need to provision the VPN capability between the two endpoints (yours and Amazon's).

12. Please note that once this step is completed, charging will commence for your Amazon VPC service.

13. Once all of the steps have been completed, your VPC screen in the AWS Console should look like the following screenshot:

14. After all the steps mentioned earlier have been completed, the **Download Configuration** button will become available. Clicking on this will download all of the configuration information that your enterprise will require to configure the VPN connection for your side.

15. At this time, the configuration files provided are already configured for Cisco and Juniper series routers:

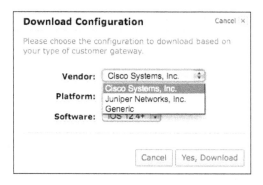

16. If your enterprise does not have one of the named routers, a **Generic** option is provided.

Starting servers in your VPC

Once your Amazon VPC has been created, starting an EC2 instance in your VPC is quite straightforward. When creating a new EC2 instance, you will note the following option in the **Request Instance Wizard**:

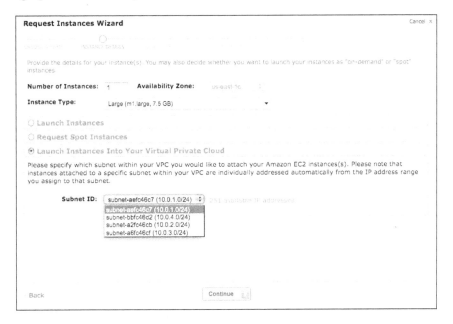

The subnets that we created earlier are now available as an option in the **Launch Instances Into Your Virtual Private Cloud**.

 One important point you may notice from the previous screenshot is that you no longer have the opportunity to choose the **Availability Zone** that your server will run in, this option is grayed out and set when you configured your VPC.

Also, you will note that there is now an option for you to enter an IP address on the **Instance Details** dialog, if you don't add an IP address here, one will be allocated for you:

 Please note, that only one availability zone is available to your VPC.

AWS elastic load balancing

AWS **Elastic Load Balancing (ELB)** is used to distribute traffic between one or more EC2 instances in AWS. We looked at AWS load balancing briefly in *Chapter 2, Mapping your Enterprise Requirements Against Amazon's Offerings*. One of the interesting things about ELB is its ability to distribute traffic across multiple availability zones within the same region; however, at this point, ELB does not scale across separate regions.

1. Setting up an ELB is relatively straightforward. The first thing to do is create the actual AWS ELB instance in the AWS console.

 By default, Apache Web Server is already configured on port 80.

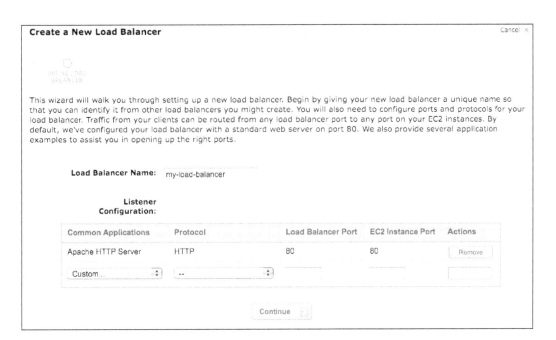

2. The next step is configuring the health check for the ELB. By default the health check uses the HTTP protocol on port 80 to GET the /index.html web page. If this page is unavailable for any reason, then the EC2 instance is flagged as unavailable.

3. For Microsoft **Internet Information Server (IIS)**, the default start page is actually **/iisstart.htm**, so change the ping path to this if you are starting with default IIS:

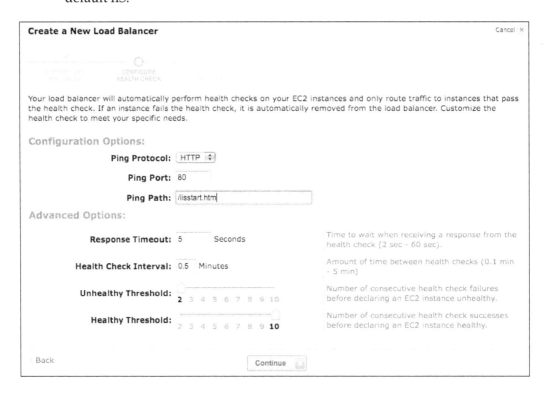

4. The advanced options are used to determine how often to check and how many times. One thing you will note from the defaults is that it only takes two failed tests to flag an instance as unhealthy, but it takes 10 successful tests to flag an instance as healthy, so by default it will take at least 10 seconds before an EC2 instance is flagged as unhealthy and traffic is stopped from being directed to it.

5. Once the health check details have been selected, you will be prompted for the instances that you would like added. Note that these are running EC2 instances, so when an instance is terminated and restarted, that new EC2 instance will not automatically be a member of the ELB.

 Terminating an instance will remove it from an Elastic Load Balancer, starting an instance will not automatically add it to an ELB.

One thing to be aware of is that when load balancing across availability zones, ELB will load balance *equally* across the zones, independent of how many EC2 instances are running in each zone.

 Be sure to have the same number of EC2 instances in each availability zone when using an ELB to distribute the load across zones.

Using ELB for HTTPS

When configuring ELB, you will need to make the decision to either have your ELB instance manage the SSL certificates and decrypt your HTTPS traffic, or have your ELB instance pass the HTTPS traffic through to your IIS instances to decrypt.

To configure the ELB instance to manage HTTPS for you, all that is required is to add HTTPS as a protocol in the **Define Load Balancer** dialog of the **Create a New Load Balancer** wizard. If the HTTPS protocol has been added, you will be presented with the following dialog after clicking on the **Continue** button:

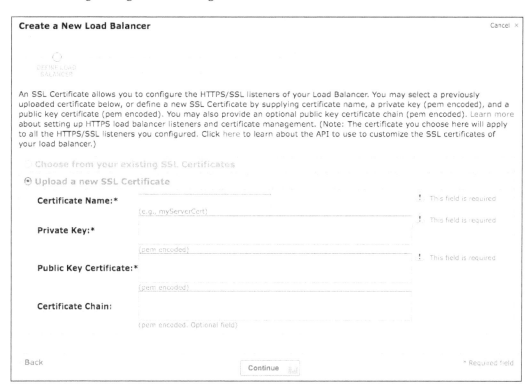

When configuring your ELB instance to manage HTTPS, you will need to upload both the **Private Key** and the **Public Key Certificate**. Once this has been done, any HTTPS traffic directed to external port 443 on your ELB instance will be decrypted and then re-directed to port 80 (HTTP) on your internal IIS web server instances:

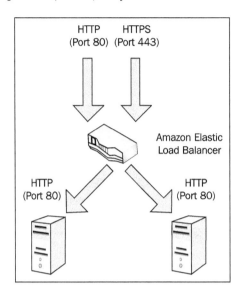

Amazon CloudFront networking

Amazon CloudFront is a technology provided by Amazon to enable caching of content on edge locations distributed around the world to provide low latency access for client browsers. CloudFront can be incredibly useful in improving performance for your website, even if it is only caching simple things such as your company logo and perhaps some static images.

CloudFront achieves this by using some smart redirection under the bonnet whenever a user accesses a static file stored in S3. If the file that they are attempting to access is part of a CloudFront distribution, AWS will redirect the GET request to a location closer to the end user, which is part of the CloudFront network.

There are currently 10 CloudFront edge locations in the U.S., four in Europe, and three in Asia:

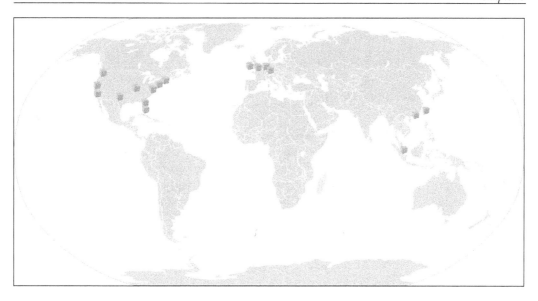

To see how this works, let's follow these steps and take a look at the next diagram:

1. A user (+) in Europe accesses a website hosted on AWS in Virginia (**us-east**).

2. The html for the website is returned to the browser from the originating website.

3. The images and other CloudFront data are returned from the edge location nearby rather than the web server located in the U.S.

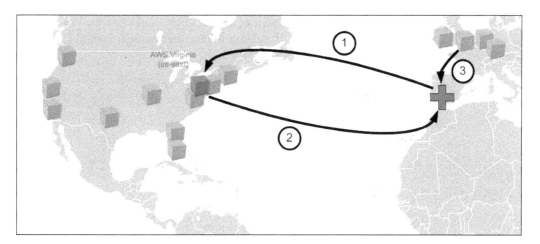

If the file is not yet cached at that CloudFront location, AWS will get the file from the original location and cache it when satisfying the request.

 You will need to activate the CloudFront service prior to using it.

Prior to setting up CloudFront, you will need to create an S3 bucket that is domain name-compatible, so it may only have lower case letters and underscores as part of its name. Once the bucket has been created, you will need to change the permissions on the bucket to allow **Everyone** view access. To do this, right-click on the bucket and select **Properties**. Add the permission **View Permissions** to the **Grantee: Everyone**:

Now that you have a bucket ready to go, add the images and other files to this bucket that you would like cached by CloudFront. You can start by just adding your company logo and any other images, that are located on your website.

Once you have uploaded these to your new S3 bucket, you will need to create a distribution. A distribution connects an existing S3 bucket with the CloudFront service. To do this, select **CloudFront** in the **AWS Console** and click on the **Create Distribution** button. You will see the following dialog:

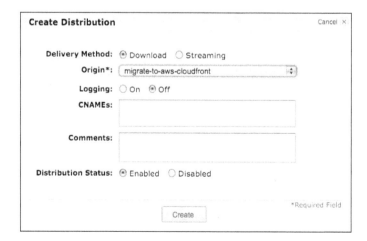

To create the distribution, select the **Delivery Method** of **Download**, and select your S3 bucket from the **Origin** drop-down list. This distribution will be used to serve static files. To serve streaming media such as video, select the **Streaming** option, you will need to create different distributions for pictures and video.

The **CNAMEs** box is used if you would like a specific domain name for your distribution, rather than an automatically generated domain name. It will become more obvious as to why this may be necessary in a moment.

Once your distribution has been created, take note of the **Domain Name**. This is what you will use to reference your CloudFront files from your website:

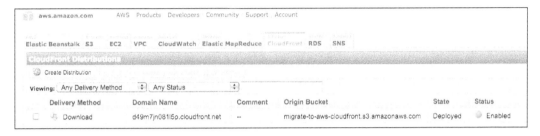

In the previous example, the domain that has been allocated by AWS is **d49m7jn08115p.cloudfront.net**. So to reference a file called `logo.png` that is located in your S3 bucket, you would use the following syntax:

```
http://d49m7jn08115p.cloudfront.net/logo.png
```

As you can see, the URL for your CloudFront logo does not contain the name of your website domain. If you would like to explicitly state the URL that will be used, then you can create a CNAME record and point it to the AWS-generated domain name, as shown in the previous screenshot. Once the CNAME has been created, edit the CloudFront distribution and enter your CNAME into the **CNAMEs** textbox.

Once this is done, you will be able to use your own domain when pointing to CloudFront resources.

After configuring the CloudFront resources, you will need to modify your website image URLs to point to the CloudFront URL, rather than the static local URL.

Setting up the networking for our sample application

Now that we are clear as to how Amazon does networking, let's look at how we can apply that to our sample application:

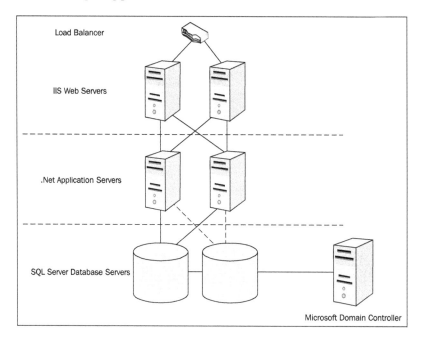

The database layer

As you can see, in this layer we have a domain controller managing two SQL Server database instances. The domain controller in our sample application is a standalone domain controller and is not part of an enterprise domain. The reason we have a domain controller is purely to manage the security for the two SQL Server instances, as SQL Server is poor at managing security outside a domain:

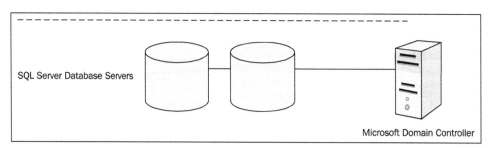

So in this case, we have two servers, which need to be part of a domain, and as we saw earlier in this chapter, when servers in AWS need to be part of a domain they must have Elastic IP addresses added.

So the first thing to do is to add an elastic IP address to both the SQL Server EC2 instances as well as the Domain controller instance.

In this example, the IP addresses are:

Server Name	Elastic IP Address
Domain Controller:	50.16.185.14
Database Server #1	50.16.236.164
Database Server #2	50.16.221.13

Once each of the database servers has an elastic IP address added, edit the Domain Controllers Security Group, and add the elastic IP address allocated to each of the database servers with the UDP and TCP protocols:

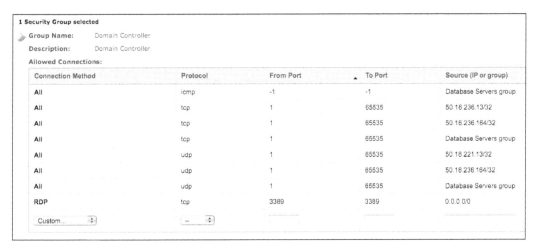

In the previous case, the **Domain Controller Security Group** has the two IP addresses **50.16.236.164** and **50.16.221.13** added using both UDP and TCP.

Once you have done this, log in to each of your database server instances and modify the DNS settings to point to the Elastic IP address allocated to the domain controller:

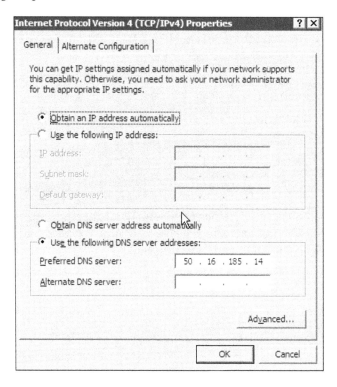

Now that we have completed the groundwork, we will be able to add our database's servers to the domain on our domain controller.

 Make sure you have either disabled Windows firewall or modified it to reflect the security group settings (mentioned earlier) as well or you will not be able to add the servers to the domain.

So now, for each of the database servers, add them to the domain as you would normally; however, do not change their names, as this will cause issues for SQL server later on.

Now we have the networking for our database layer complete. We have two database servers connected to a local domain (the domain is standalone in AWS). We will configure these database servers in the next chapter.

The application server layer

In the application server layer for our sample application, we have two application servers:

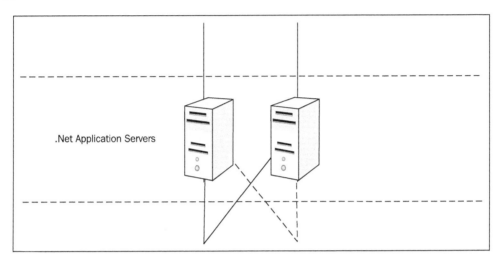

Each of these communicates with the designated database server and is referenced by its designated web server. Each application server will connect to the database servers using **Microsoft Data Access Components (MDAC 2.6)**. Because there is no need for each of the application servers to communicate with each other, there is no need to add them to their own security group. Each server, however, will be required to allow access to port 80 from the web servers.

So the first step is to add an Elastic IP address to each of the application servers; these are the elastic IP addresses used for this example.

Server Name	Elastic IP Address
Application Server #1	184.73.175.58
Application Server #2	184.73.223.216

Once this has been done, modify the **App Servers** security group to allow access from the **Web Servers** security group.

 If you are using the AWS console, you will note that you are unable to restrict the ports when adding a security group to the source address field.

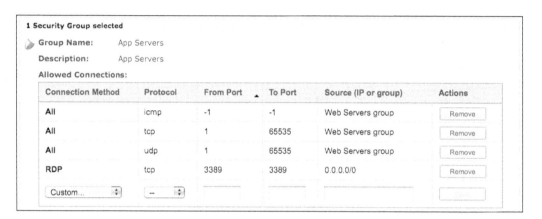

1 Security Group selected

Group Name: App Servers

Description: App Servers

Allowed Connections:

Connection Method	Protocol	From Port	To Port	Source (IP or group)	Actions
All	icmp	-1	-1	Web Servers group	Remove
All	tcp	1	65535	Web Servers group	Remove
All	udp	1	65535	Web Servers group	Remove
RDP	tcp	3389	3389	0.0.0.0/0	Remove
Custom...	--				

By default the AWS console adds all of the ports.

If this is too relaxed for your security policy, then you can use the AWS command-line tools to refine this. To allow just port 80, use the following AWS command instead:

```
C:\AWS>ec2-authorize "App Servers" -P tcp -p 80 -o "Web Servers" -u
764516644405
```

(The –u option is now required and is your Amazon account ID)

 Please note, once a security rule has been added from the command-line tools, it can only be removed using the command-line tools.

To remove this rule, the opposite command can be run:

```
C:\AWS>ec2-revoke "App Servers" -P tcp -p 80 -o "Web Servers" -u
764516644405
```

So the App Server security group will now look like this instead:

Connection Method	Protocol	From Port	To Port	Source (IP or group)	Actions
1 Security Group selected					
Group Name: App Servers					
Description: App Servers					
Allowed Connections:					
RDP	tcp	3389	3389	0.0.0.0/0	Remove
HTTP	tcp	80	80	Web Servers group	Remove
Custom...	--				

Now that the **App Servers** security group has been modified, you will need to go back to the **Database Servers** security group and allow Port **1433** from the **App Servers** security group. Once again, this will need to be done from the command line. The command for doing this is:

```
c:\AWS>ec2-authorize "Database Servers" -P tcp -p 1433 -o "App Servers"
-u 764516644405
```

So now the **Database Servers** security group will look like the following:

Connection Method	Protocol	From Port	To Port	Source (IP or group)	Actions
1 Security Group selected					
Group Name: Database Servers					
Description: Database Servers					
Allowed Connections:					
All	icmp	-1	-1	Database Servers group	Remove
All	tcp	1	65535	Database Servers group	Remove
All	udp	1	65535	Database Servers group	Remove
MS SQL Server	tcp	1433	1433	App Servers group	Remove
RDP	tcp	3389	3389	0.0.0.0/0	Remove
Custom...	--				

The web server layer

In our web server layer, we have two web servers servicing an AWS load balancer:

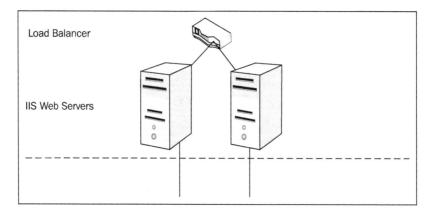

Load Balancer

IIS Web Servers

Since these servers are never accessed directly (they are accessed via the load balancer) there is no need to allocate an elastic IP address to these two servers. However, we do need to allow access to everyone on Port 80. As this does not involve another security group as the source, it can be done directly from the AWS Console:

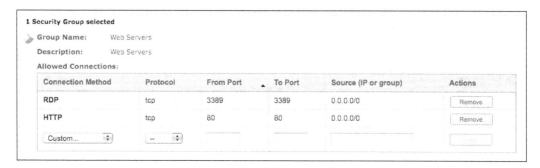

1 Security Group selected

Group Name: Web Servers
Description: Web Servers

Allowed Connections:

Connection Method	Protocol	From Port	To Port	Source (IP or group)	Actions
RDP	tcp	3389	3389	0.0.0.0/0	Remove
HTTP	tcp	80	80	0.0.0.0/0	Remove
Custom...	--				

Note that the Source (IP or Group) for the RDP protocol would normally be restricted to the IP address of our Enterprise, for example, (X.X.X.X/32).

This concludes the network configuration for our sample application!

Summary

In this chapter, we have covered the basics of networking in AWS. We looked at Amazon Elastic IPs, Amazon Elastic Load balancing, and Amazon Virtual Private Clouds. We also looked at how we set up a standalone **Active Directory Domain Controller** (**DC**) in AWS and how to overcome the issues with DCs and Security Groups. We saw in detail how to set up an application in AWS, and the step-by-step procedure on how to set up our sample application networking.

In the next chapter, we will look at how to set up our database servers for our sample application, as well as looking at the following AWS services:

- Amazon vendor-specific AMIs
- Amazon Relational Database Service (RDS)
- Amazon Elastic MapReduce
- Amazon SimpleDB

6
Putting Databases in the Cloud

There are many options to choose from while making the decision to migrate an application based on Microsoft technologies to the Amazon cloud. More than likely, the current database will be SQL Server or Oracle. Initially, it makes sense to keep the infrastructure the same and minimize the changes and disruption caused by migrating an application to AWS, so the first part of this chapter deals exclusively with Microsoft SQL Server and Oracle. However, there are long-term benefits in looking at other database options and technology that could be used to complement your application.

In this chapter, we will look at not only using the existing vendor-specific AMIs to provide database services, but also at the services provided by Amazon directly, such as **SimpleDB** and the **Relational Database Service (RDS)**.

Examining SQL Server

In this section, we will detail step-by-step on how to set up and manage an SQL Server 2008 Standard instance in AWS. This will include the setting up and configuration of SQL server as well as the import and backup of data.

SQL Server AMI

It is important to note that you may not provide your own licenses of SQL Server to run in AWS, nor can you install SQL Server onto a blank Windows Server AMI and buy new licenses. You must use the SQL Server AMIs provided by Amazon.

Amazon provides the following AMIs pre-loaded with SQL Server. These are the AMI IDs and descriptions as provided by Amazon in the Amazon Machine Images Library at: `http://aws.amazon.com/amis/AWS?c=25&p=1&sm=dD`

AMI ID	Notes
ami-69c32f00	**SQL Express**
	Windows Server 2008 32-bit with SQL Server 2008 Express + IIS + ASP.NET.
	The image contains Microsoft Windows 2008 Datacenter R1 SP2 32-bit with SQL 2008 Express pre-installed on an `AMI backed by Amazon EBS`.
	IIS 7.0 and ASP.NET roles have been enabled by default.
ami-63c32f0a	**SQL Express**
	Windows Server 2008 64-bit with SQL Server 2008 Express + IIS + ASP.NET.
	The image contains Microsoft Windows 2008 Datacenter R1 SP2 64-bit with SQL 2008 Express pre-installed on an `AMI backed by Amazon EBS`.
	This image has IIS 7.0 enabled with ASP.NET components installed.
ami-2bc32f42	**SQL Standard 2008**
	Windows Server 2008 with SQL Server 2008 Standard.
	The image contains Microsoft Windows 2008 Datacenter R1 SP2 64-bit with Microsoft SQL 2008 Standard pre-installed on an `AMI backed by Amazon EBS`.
	This Windows AMI should be used as a starting point for your 64-bit Windows 2008 SQL Servers.
ami-0535d66c	**SQL Standard 2005**
	Windows Server 2003 R2 and SQL Server 2005 Standard (64-bit).
	The image contains Microsoft SQL-Server Standard installed on Windows 2003 R2 DataCenter Anonymous.
	This Windows-AMI should be used as a starting point for your 64-bit Windows SQL-Servers.
ami-d920c3b0	**SQL Express**
	Windows Server 2003 R2 and SQL Server Express + IIS + ASP.NET (64-bit).
	The image contains Microsoft SQL-Server Express + IIS + ASP.NET installed on Windows 2003 R2 DataCenter Anonymous 64-bit Edition.

As you can see from the previous table, Amazon provides exactly one AMI for SQL Server 2005, and exactly one AMI for SQL Server 2008. Both of these are standard editions. The remainders are SQL Server Express editions.

It is worth noting that Microsoft in general provides the following editions of SQL Server:

- SQL Server Express
- SQL Server Workgroup
- SQL Server Web
- SQL Server Standard
- SQL Server Enterprise
- SQL Server Datacenter

Of which only two are represented by Amazon AMIs, (SQL Server Standard and SQL Server Express).

This effectively means that any SQL Server instances running in Amazon are restricted to SQL Server Standard as their maximum available edition.

 At this point in time Amazon does not support migrating your own existing licenses of SQL Server to AWS.

The restrictions of this become quite apparent when we compare the various editions of SQL Server 2008.

Here are some summarized key differences between Enterprise, Standard, and Express.

Feature	Enterprise *** Not available on AWS	Standard	Express
Number of CPUs	8	4	1
Max memory	2 TB	64 GB	1 GB
Max database size	524PB	524PB	10 GB
Database mirroring support	Yes, both asynchronous and synchronous	Yes, synchronous only	No
Log shipping	Yes	Yes	No
Database encryption	Yes	No	No
Backup and maintenance plans	Yes	Yes	No
Email alerts	Yes	Yes	No
Management console	Yes	Yes	No

Immediately we can see that there are issues with this. SQL Server 2008 Standard Edition supports a maximum of four CPUs, which means that running the Amazon SQL Server Standard AMI on a "High-Memory Quadruple Extra Large Instance" (eight virtual CPUs) or a "High-CPU Extra Large Instance" (eight virtual CPUs) would mean that SQL Server would use only 50 percent of the virtual CPUs provisioned to that EC2 instance.

 Do not use High-Memory Quadruple Extra Large Instance or High-CPU Extra Large Instances to run the SQL Server Standard AMI.

SQL Server costs

The costs for running SQL server in AWS vary depending on which of the two versions supplied by Amazon you choose to use. SQL Server Express is free to use, you only pay for the cost of the Windows AMI and the instance cost.

However, costs for SQL Server Standard are around double the cost of the base Windows AMI. Here are the prices:

US – N. Virginia	US – N. California	EU – Ireland	APAC – Singapore
Standard Instances	**Windows Usage**	**Windows and SQL Server Usage**	
Small (Default)	$0.12 per hour	---	
Large	$0.48 per hour	$1.08 per hour	
Extra Large	$0.96 per hour	$1.56 per hour	
Micro Instances	**Windows Usage**	**Windows and SQL Server Usage**	
Micro	$0.03 per hour	---	
High-Memory Instances	**Windows Usage**	**Windows and SQL Server Usage**	
Extra Large	$0.62 per hour	$1.22 per hour	
Double Extra Large	$1.24 per hour	$1.84 per hour	
Quadruple Extra Large	$2.48 per hour	$3.68 per hour	
High-CPU Instances	**Windows Usage**	**Windows and SQL Server Usage**	
Medium	$0.29 per hour	---	
Extra Large	$1.16 per hour	$2.36 per hour	

To calculate the costings for each version, use the **Windows Usage** column to calculate the cost of using the free SQL Server Express instance and use the **Windows and SQL Server Usage** column to calculate the SQL Server Standard usage costs.

Amazon does not support using SQL Server AMIs together with reserved instances at this time. This means that usage costs are calculated using **On-Demand** instance costings.

 This means that any already purchased reserved instances may not be used to run SQL Server AMIs.

To understand these costs, let's look at the cost of running a SQL Server 2008 Standard instance for one year on a Standard Large Instance. (Two virtual CPUs) The cost for this is 1.08 dollars/hour or 0.60 dollar/hour more than the standard windows instance. If we multiply that 0.60 dollar out over a year we get 438 dollars/month or 5,256 dollars/year.

Compare that with the pricing located on the Microsoft Pricing page located at:

```
http://www.microsoft.com/sqlserver/en/us/get-sql-server/how-to-buy.
aspx.
```

Pricing for a full CPU license of SQL Server 2008 Standard is, 7171 dollars per CPU license. For two CPUs this becomes 14,342 dollars. So break even is around three years. In my opinion, this is obviously good value.

However, what is not as obvious is that SQL Server 2008 Web Edition costs are substantially different. On the Microsoft website, the cost for SQL Server Web Edition is 3,500 dollars per CPU, or 7,000 dollars for two CPUs. However, if you opt for a Service Provider License Agreement (SPLA) license model, the cost of the Web Edition of SQL Server drops to 15 dollars/month, or 30 dollars/month for two CPUs.

(All pricing is in US dollars)

It is clear from this discussion that although the costs for SQL Server are relatively cheap on AWS, they could be substantially cheaper if AWS were willing to offer a broader range of SQL Server editions on AWS.

So, in summary, if you would like to use SQL Server on AWS, you will need to note the following points:

1. You *may not* migrate your existing SQL Server licenses to AWS.
2. You *may not* purchase new licenses to use on AWS that are not provided by Amazon.
3. You *must* use the provided AWS AMIs and the associated bundled costing model.
4. Only SQL Server Standard and SQL Server Express are available on AWS.

5. You *may not* use **Reserved Instances** to run SQL Server AMIs.

6. SQL Server Standard AMIs are limited to *four* virtual CPUs.

Setting up SQL Server

In this section, we will be setting up the SQL Server:

1. To set up an SQL Server Standard instance, select the **Microsoft SQL Server on Windows Server 2008** AMI and start up a **Large** (m1.large) instance on EC2.

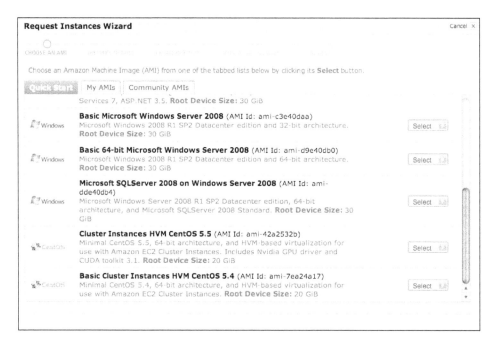

2. Once the instance has started, right-click on it and retrieve the password in the AWS console using the key pair that you selected when you started the instance.

 Remember to wait at least 15 minutes for the encrypted password to appear in your new EC2 instance log.

3. Then connect to your new instance.

4. Once connected as administrator to your new SQL Server EC2 instance, the first task is to start the SQL Server Configuration Manager.

5. Select the **SQL Server Services** node in the left-hand window and you will notice that all of the SQL Server services are stopped and disabled.

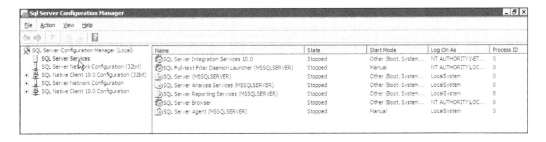

For a minimum operating instance of SQL Server, I recommend that you set the following services to Auto and start them:

SQL Server (MSSQLSERVER)

SQL Server Agent (MSSQLSERVER)

SQL Server Browser (MSSQLSERVER)

6. To do this, double-click on each one in turn to change the **Start Mode** on the **Service** tab to **Automatic**.

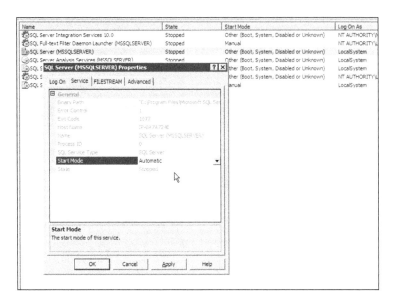

7. Click on **Apply** and then start the service on the **Log On** tab.

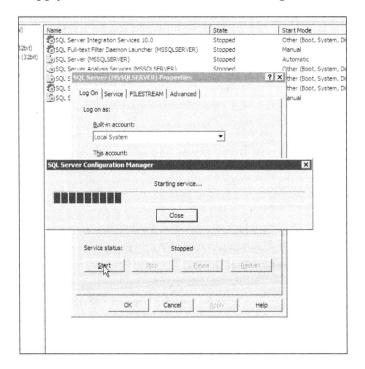

8. Once this step is complete, SQL server will be up and running on your EC2 instance.

Managing the SQL Server

Now that SQL Server is up and running, run the **Microsoft SQL Server Management Studio** from the **Microsoft SQL Server 2008** group in the start menu.

1. You will be able to log on by clicking on the **Connect** button as the administrator has already been added by default as a SQL Server System admin.

2. You now have access to all of the standard SQL server management tools available for SQL Server.

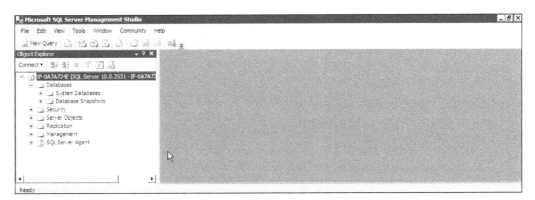

Connecting to SQL Server

To ensure that you always connect to the correct instance of SQL Server, I strongly recommend that you allocate an Elastic IP address to any new instances. Once you have allocated a new Elastic IP, use the Public DNS in the connection string. As we discussed in *Chapter 5, Amazon's Approach to Networking* this will resolve to the internal IP address, which is allocated at the time to your EC2 instance.

Integrated security versus mixed mode security

By default, the Microsoft SQL Server Instance is set up to use integrated security only; however, depending on whether you will configure a domain controller for your SQL Server instance, you may need to change this to **Mixed Mode Security**.

Microsoft does not consider changing the security model to mixed mode best practice, so it is preferable to install and configure a domain controller if at all possible to support your SQL Server instance. If this is not practicable, to change the security model, right-click on the root server name node of your database instance in SQL Management Studio and select **Properties**. You will be presented with the following:

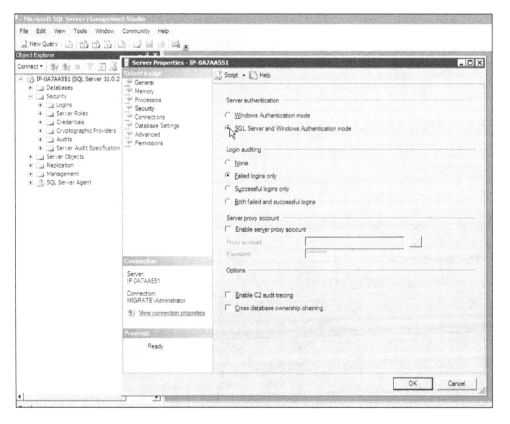

Select the **Security** option in the left-hand window and click on the **SQL Server and Windows Authentication mode** radio button, and click on **OK**.

> You will need to restart the SQL Server before the changes take effect.

Windows firewall

Also by default, the windows firewall is set to block all incoming connections on port 1433, which is the default port for a SQL Server instance. To allow connections to this instance, please configure the windows firewall by adding a custom port exception.

To do this, select the **Windows Firewall** icon in the **Control Panel**. Now click on **Change Settings**, select **Exceptions** then click on the **Add Port** button.

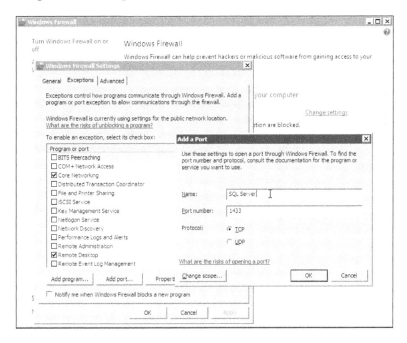

Enter the name **SQL Server** for the **Name** and **1433** for the **Port number**, and click **OK**.

> If you still have trouble connecting to SQL Server, check the settings in your security group assigned to your database and make sure port 1433 has been opened.

Importing data to the SQL instance

Now that we are able to connect to our SQL Server instance, we will need to create a database and import data into it. In *Chapter 4, How Storage Works on Amazon*, we looked at how we move bulk data into the cloud using the AWS Import/Export service. Using this service, we saw how to move large amounts of data into an S3 storage bucket.

However, if our initial data is much smaller, then we can copy our data directly to S3, and from there, import it into our new database server. To do this, we can use the same S3 utility that we described in *Chapter 4, How Storage Works on Amazon*.

So to start, make sure you have a current backup of your SQL Server database you would like to import.

> For information on SQL Server 2008 backup and restore procedures, please refer to the following reference from Microsoft MSDN:

```
http://technet.microsoft.com/en-us/library/ms187048.aspx.
```

Install and configure the S3 tools as described in *Chapter 4, How Storage Works on Amazon* and run the following command:

```
C:\AWS> s3 put /big:1 /nogui <bucket name> <SQL Server backup
  file>
```

Where <bucket name> is the name of the S3 destination bucket, and **<SQL Server backup file>** is the name of the backup file that you would like to import into your new SQL Server instance in the cloud.

For example, to copy the file **c:\data\backup\example_full.bak** to the **migrate_to_aws** bucket use the following command:

```
C:\AWS> s3 put /big:1 /nogui migrate_to_aws c:\data\backup\example_full.bak
```

```
C:\Windows\system32\cmd.exe

c:\AWS>s3 put /big:1 /nogui migrate_to_aws_backup c:\data\Backup\example_full.bak
s3.exe version 1.7 - check for updates at http://s3.codeplex.com

example_full.bak.000
example_full.bak.001
example_full.bak.002

c:\AWS>_
```

The **/big:1** syntax instructs the program to split the file into manageable 1 MB chunks, so the upload can be resume after an interruption.

Now that your backup file is up on S3, reverse the procedure to copy it to your new SQL Server instance.

Alternatively, you can use the AWS Console to copy the backup file to S3, and use the reverse to copy it from S3 to a local directory (`c:\data\backup`) on your new SQL Server instance.

 Please read the following section on how to configure your new instance to run the AWS Console.

Once the backup file has been uploaded onto your new SQL Server EC2 instance, then restore from the backup file. Your data is now available on the new SQL Server instance.

Using the AWS console on your new SQL Server instance

Using the AWS Console directly on an EC2 Windows instance is not recommended; however, to enable the console to operate correctly, you will need to disable **Internet Explorer Enhanced Security Configuration**. To do this, run **Server Manager** and select **Configure IE ESC** in the **Server Summary** section.

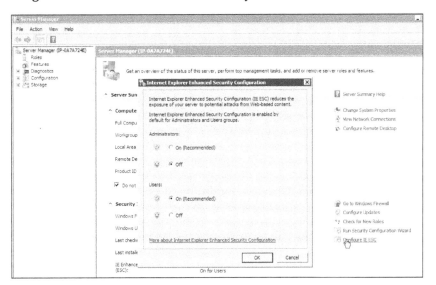

Select **Off** for **Administrators** and click on **OK**.

Oracle

In this section, we will detail step-by-step on how to set up and manage an Oracle Standard instance in AWS. This will include the setting up and configuration of Oracle as well as the import and backup of data.

Oracle AMIs

Oracle does not supply a bundled AMI complete with bundled charging like Microsoft does with SQL Server. Instead Oracle supplies existing AMIs without bundled pricing and supports the transfer of your new or existing licenses to Oracle instances running in EC2 on AWS.

While this approach does mean it is more complex to set up initially, the flexibility gained under this model to install the version of Oracle that best fits your needs is well worth the little bit of extra work!

 To run Oracle in AWS you must provide your own Oracle licenses.

All of the Oracle pre-built AMIs—as supplied by Oracle—are configured to run on Oracle Enterprise Linux Release 5. There are no pre-built AMIs as supplied by Oracle at this time configured to run under the Windows operating system.

To see the full list of Oracle AMIs, please refer to the following link:

`http://aws.amazon.com/amis/Oracle`.

 Note that unlike Microsoft, Oracle does not require you to use a pre-built AMI. So if you would like to start with a base image of Windows and install your own version of Oracle on this, then Oracle will still allow you to use your existing licensing.

Licensing

Licensing for Oracle on AWS has been documented by Oracle in `www.oracle.com/us/corporate/pricing/cloud-licensing-070579.pdf`.

For the purpose of calculating the number of processor licenses required in AWS, the following table can be used:

Name	Max number of EC2 CPUs	Number of CPUs (rounded) to convert to a full processor license	Example EC2 instance size	Number of processor licenses required
Oracle Enterprise	unlimited	Divide by 2	Extra Large	2
			(four virtual cores)	
			Large	1
			(two virtual cores)	
			Small	1
			(one virtual core)	
Oracle Standard	16	Divide by 4	Extra Large	1
			(four virtual cores)	
			Large	1
			(two virtual cores)	
			Small	1
			(one virtual core)	
Oracle Standard One	8	Divide by 4	Extra Large	1
			(four virtual cores)	
			Large	1
			(two virtual cores)	
			Small	1
			(one virtual core)	

So, in summary if you would like to use Oracle on AWS, you will need to note the following points:

1. You *may* migrate your existing Oracle licenses to AWS.
2. You *may* purchase new licenses to use on AWS that are not provided by Amazon.
3. You are *not required* to use the provided AWS AMIs.
4. Oracle Standard, Standard One, and Enterprise are available on AWS.
5. You *may* use **Reserved Instances** to run SQL Server AMIs.
6. Oracle Standard AMIs scale to sixteen virtual CPUs.

Setting up Oracle

To set up Oracle, select a version of Oracle that suites your needs. It is important to match your version or Oracle with the correct instance size in AWS. In our case, we will be selecting the Oracle Standard Edition One 64-bit version and running in on a Large EC2 instance, which will require one processor license.

 The first time you start your Oracle instance up it may take up to 15 minutes to start.

1. To continue the set up of Oracle, we will need to connect to the new Oracle EC2 instance using **SSH**. If you are using a Linux or Mac OSX desktop then SSH is already installed, if you are using a windows desktop, then you will need to download a SSH client.

 I recommend using **PuTTY**, a free SSH client for Windows located at:
`http://www.chiark.greenend.org.uk/~sgtatham/putty/download.html`.

2. However, you may use any client that is SSH-compatible. For this example, we will be using PuTTY.

 More information is available on PuTTY on the Amazon website located at:
`http://docs.amazonwebservices.com/AmazonEC2/gsg/2007-01-19/putty.html`.

3. Download the `putty.exe` and `puttygen.exe` from the location mentioned earlier and place it into your `C:\AWS` disk directory alongside your other AWS tools. You will need `puttygen.exe` to convert the key-pair file used by AWS into a format that is compatible with putty.

4. Next, launch `puttygen.exe`.

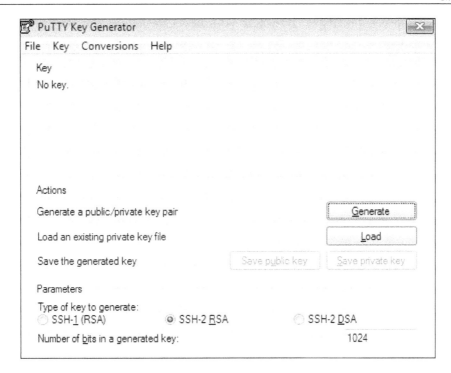

5. Click on the **Load** button and select your existing AWS key-pair file. You will be presented with the following:

6. Follow the previous directions and click on the **Save private key** button and save it with the same name but with the .ppk extension in the C:\AWS directory.

7. Now you are ready to connect to your new Oracle instance. Right-click on your new instance in the AWS Console and select the **Connect** option, you will be presented with the following:

8. Copy the command line and paste it into a command prompt. Now edit the **ssh** part and replace it with **putty**, and replace the **.pem** extension with the **.ppk** extension.

```
C:\AWS> putty -i migrate_to_aws_key_pair.ppk root@ec2-50-16-24-
150.compute-1.amazonaws.com
```

 To make this easier, you can rename `putty.exe` to `ssh.exe` and rename your key pair file from `<name>.pem` to `<name>.ppk`. Then you will be able to copy and paste the connection string without modification.

9. This will start the connection process with your Oracle instance.

10. Before connecting, putty will warn you that the RSA fingerprint does not match an existing fingerprint, click on **Yes** to accept the new fingerprint.

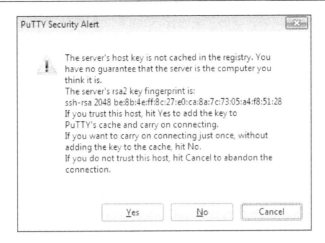

11. Once connected to your new Oracle instance, you will be able to continue the installation and configuration of your new Oracle database.

12. The first thing you will be asked to do is accept the Oracle end user license agreement:

    ```
    To accept the agreements, enter 'y', otherwise enter 'n'.

    Do you accept? [y/n]: y

    Thank you.

    You may now use this machine.
    ```

13. Next you will be prompted to enter a new password for the **oracle** user;

    ```
    Please set the oracle operating system password.

    Changing password for user oracle.

    New UNIX password:*****
    ```

14. Next you will be asked if you would like to create a new database:

    ```
    Would you like to create a database now [y|n]:   y
    ```

15. Next you will be asked where you would like to create your new database. It is recommended that Oracle databases be created on independent EBS volumes and that a separate EBS volume be used for the data and flash recovery areas. However, for this example, I will be selecting the default location on the local drive:

    ```
    Option [1] Use Default:
    ```

16. Next you will be asked to give your Oracle database a name, by default this is usually ORCL.

```
Please enter the name for your Oracle Database.
This name will be used as your
ORACLE SID (System Identifier):  ORCL
```

17. Next enter passwords for all of the Oracle admin accounts.

```
SYS (Database Administrative Account) Password:
Confirm SYS password:
SYSTEM (Database Administrative Account) Password:
Confirm SYSTEM password:
DBSNMP (Enterprise Manager Administrative Account) Password:
Confirm DBSNMP password:
SYSMAN (Enterprise Manager Administrative Account) Password:
Confirm SYSMAN password:
ADMIN (Applications Express Administrative Account) Password:
Confirm ADMIN password:
```

18. Now that you have supplied the required information, your Oracle instance will be created. This will take up to 15 minutes to complete.

19. When your Oracle instance has been created, you will be prompted with: **Welcome to the Oracle Secure Backup Cloud Module Installation**

20. At this point you may cancel the remainder of the setup, as this is related to creating a backup plan for your new database. This may be completed at any time from within the Enterprise Manager.

Your Oracle instance is now up and running.

Managing the Oracle instance

To ensure that you always connect to the correct instance of Oracle, I strongly recommend that you allocate an Elastic IP address to any new instances. Once you have allocated a new Elastic IP, use the Public DNS in the connection string. As we discussed in the *Chapter 5*, *Amazon's Approach to Networking*, this will resolve to the internal IP address, which is allocated at the time to your EC2 instance.

Before you connect to the **Enterprise Manager (EM)** management console for Oracle you will need to open port 1158 by adding it to the security group you added to this EC2 instance when you started it.

Then to manage your new instance, connect to enterprise manager at the following URL:

```
https://<public DNS>:1158/em
```

For example, if the public address of your new Oracle EC2 instance was:

ec2-72-44-56-190.compute-1.amazonaws.com

The URL to use would be:

```
https://ec2-72-44-56-190.compute-1.amazonaws.com:1158/em
```

Use the username of **SYS** and the password that you selected to log on to the enterprise manager console. Make sure that you connect as **SYSDBA** when you log in as **SYS**.

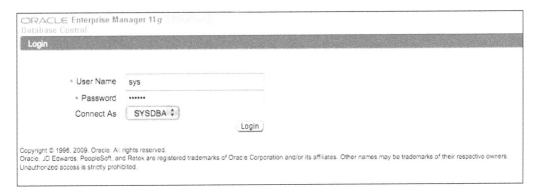

To allow connections to your new Oracle instance add port 1521 to your security group.

 Ports 1521 and 1158 are required by Oracle, so make sure these ports have been added to the security group for the Oracle instance.

You will now be able to both manage and connect to your new Oracle EC2 instance.

Importing data to the Oracle instance

Now that we are able to connect to our Oracle instance, we will need to import data into it. In *Chapter 4*, *How Storage Works on Amazon*, we looked at how we move bulk data into the cloud using the AWS Import/Export service. Using this service we saw how it was possible to move large amounts of data into a S3 storage bucket.

However, if our initial data is much smaller, then we can copy our data directly to S3, and from there, import it into our new database server. To do this, we can use the same S3 utility that we described in *Chapter 4, How Storage Works on Amazon*, if your source Oracle instance is based on Windows. If your source database is based on Linux, follow the same steps mentioned next as for our destination Oracle instance, which is running Oracle Enterprise Linux.

Because our destination Oracle instance is based on Oracle Enterprise Linux, you will need to do the following extra steps to install the S3 tools.

1. First log in to your new Oracle instance as **oracle** using **ssh**.

2. Now, run the following command to log in as root:

   ```
   $ su -
   password:
   ```

3. Once logged in as root, change to the following directory:

   ```
   $ cd /etc/yum.repos.d
   ```

4. Now run the following command to get the install package:

   ```
   $ wget http://s3tools.org/repo/CentOS_5/s3tools.repo
   ```

5. Now install it using this command:

   ```
   $ yum install s3cmd
   ```

6. Now you will need to configure it with your AWS credentials, exit from root

   $ exit

   and run the -configure command:

   ```
   $ s3cmd -configure
   Access Key: AKIAIIJXIP5XC6NW3KTQ
   Secret Key: 9UpktBlqDroY5C4Q7OnlF1pNXtK332TslYFsWy9R
   Encryption password:
   Path to GPG program [/usr/bin/gpg]:
   Use HTTPS protocol [No]:
   HTTP Proxy server name:
   ```

7. The S3cmd tools should now be configured.

8. To start, make sure you have a current backup of your Oracle database you would like to import.

For information on Oracle backup and restore procedures, please refer to the following reference from Oracle:

`http://wiki.oracle.com/page/Oracle+export+and+import+`

9. Copy the backup file up to S3 as per the instructions for importing data for SQL Server to S3.

10. Once the backup file has been copied to S3, **ssh** into your Oracle instance as the **oracle** user and run the following command to copy down your backup file.

```
$ s3cmd get s3://<bucket name>/<backup file>
```

11. For example, if your bucket was called **migrate_to_aws** and your backup file was called **example.dmp**, then the command would be:

```
$ s3cmd get s3://migrate_to_aws_backup/example.dmp
```

12. Once the backup file has been uploaded onto your new Oracle EC2 instance, then restore from the backup file.

13. Your data is now available on the new Oracle instance.

 Please note, Amazon now makes Oracle available as a RDS service as of the second quarter of 2011.

Oracle Database 11g coming to Amazon RDS
AWS plans to make Oracle Database 11g available via Amazon RDS
during the second quarter of 2011   Learn More

Other Amazon database services

While Amazon does a great job of providing AMIs for building database services, they also provide these services in a pre-packaged ready-to-use form called RDS.

Amazon RDS

We covered Amazon's **Relational Database Service (RDS)** briefly in *Chapter 2, Mapping your Enterprise Requirements Against Amazon's Offerings*. RDS is a database service provided by Amazon where they take on the management and operation of the database instance on your behalf.

In this section, we will detail how to set up an RDS instance and manage it.

Setting up the RDS service

To begin the setup, firstly you will need to sign up for the RDS Service.

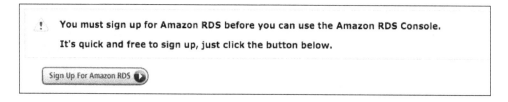

You will be prompted with the now familiar pricing page, this time for Amazon RDS. Click **Complete Sign Up** and continue.

You will need to wait for your subscription to become active; however, this only takes a minute or two.

RDS pricing

Pricing for RDS is similar to other AWS pricing, in that it is charged by the hour based on your usage. To give an indication of what RDS will cost, a **Standard On-Demand** instance will cost around 0.44 dollar/hour. Compare this with a base **Windows Standard On-Demand** instance at 0.48 dollar/hour and you can see that costings for RDS are very competitive.

Creating an RDS instance

So now that you have subscribed to the RDS service, it's time to create your first instance:

1. Once your RDS service is active, clicking on the **RDS** tab at the top of the AWS Console will bring you to the RDS management console.

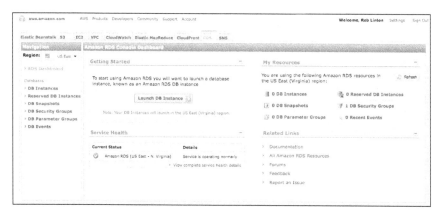

2. Click on the Launch DB Instance button to create your first DB Instance.

3. The following will be presented:

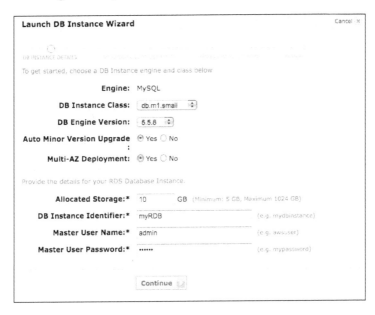

4. Select the size of your instance and the version number of **MySQL** that you would like to back your instance. In our example, we will be creating a Multi-AZ Deployment or 10 GB in size. You will also need to give your instance a name and supply the admin password.

5. The next step is to provide the database name and port details:

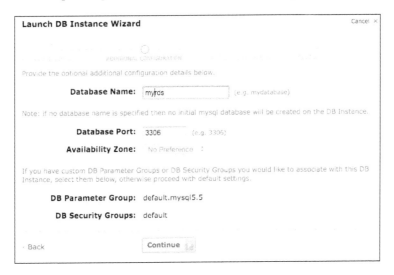

6. The database name is what is used to reference your RDS instance and is similar to a Public DNS entry.

7. Next, the Launch DB Wizard will request details regarding your backup schedule:

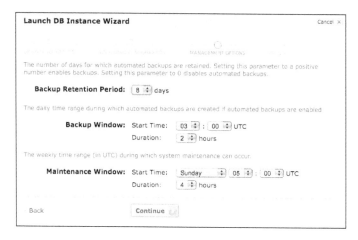

8. In the previous example, I have selected a **Backup Retention Period** of the maximum **8 days**.

9. Finally, you will be presented with the final dialog, summarizing your selections. Click **Launch DB Instance** to complete your setup:

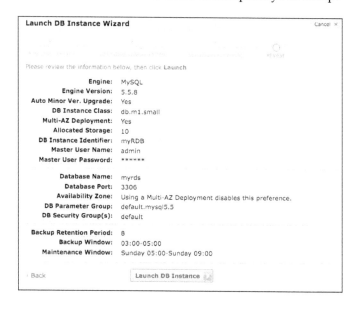

10. Your RDS instance will take a few minutes to create.

Connecting to the RDS instance

Once your RDS instance has been created select the instance and examine the details pane.

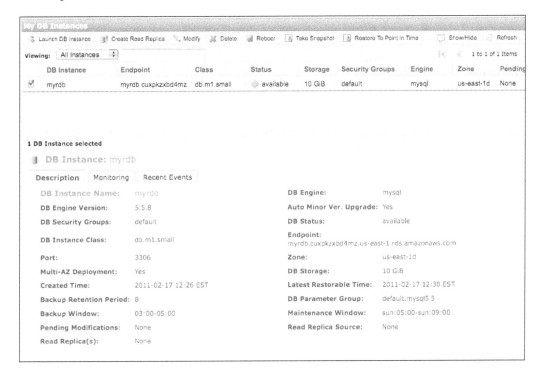

The **Endpoint** shows the address that you will use to connect to your RDS instance. In the previous example, the **Endpoint** is **myrdb.cuxpkzxbd4mz.us-east-1.rds. amazonaws.com**.

Security for RDS

Network security for RDS is managed by RDS Security groups. The management of these groups is separate from EC2 security groups, but is similar to its management.

To allow access to your new RDS instance, you will need to allow access from the client computer you will be running the management console on, as well as the EC2 instances that will be accessing this instance.

Luckily, Amazon provides methods for both of these:

1. To create a new Security Group, click on the **DB Security Groups** link in the left-hand **Navigation** window and then click on the **Create DB Security Group** button.

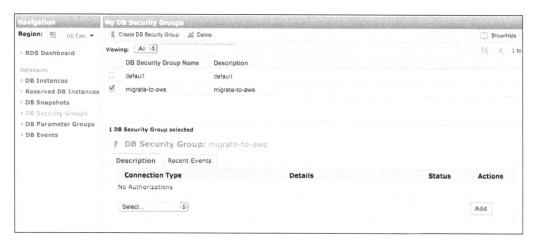

2. Give the Security Group a **Name** and **Description** and click on **Create**.
3. Once you have created your new security group, add permissions for the desktop computer you will be using as your management console.
4. Add a new CIDR/IP entry and add the IP address of the external IP of your corporate firewall to this field.

 In the following example, I have added **0.0.0.0/0**, which allows access to everyone. This is not recommended and is only for demonstration purposes.

5. Once your new RDS Security group has been created, add it to your new RDS instance.

6. To do this, select your RDS instance in the AWS Console and click on the **Yes, Modify** button.

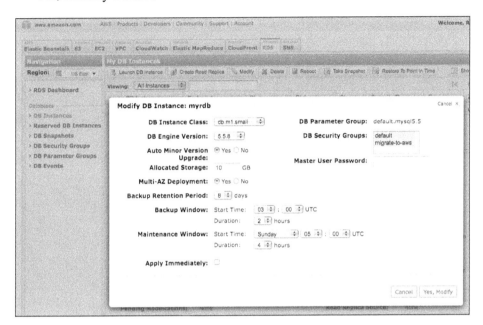

 It is now possible to use EC2 security groups for RDS, to add an EC2 security group select **EC2 Security Group** instead of **CIDR/IP** when creating the RDS security group in the **Connection Type** drop-down list.

Managing the RDS instance

To manage your new RDS instance, you may only use the tools supplied from the AWS Console.

You may modify the size of your RDS instance, the frequency of backups and take snapshots of your RDS instance that may be restored separately.

However, that is about it. RDS is designed to be virtually maintenance free, and Amazon has done a good job in achieving this.

Connect using client tools

This section focuses on connecting to your RDS instance, as it is often a point of confusion as to what configuration is required in the client to connect to your RDS instance.

1. To connect to your RDS instance, you will need to download the MySQL Workbench from:

    `http://dev.mysql.com/downloads/workbench/5.2.html`.

2. Install the workbench on your desktop computer; once installed, start the workbench:

3. Once you have run MySQL Workbench, you will be presented with the following:

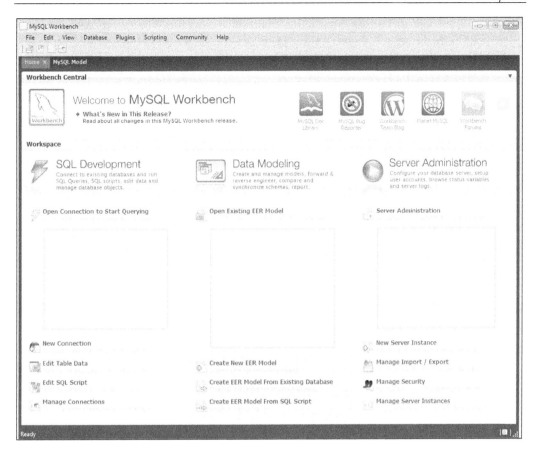

4. Click on **New Connection** and add the Endpoint that you determined previously for your new RDS instance.

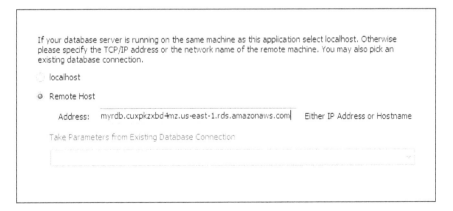

5. Click **Next** and add the same details that you added when you created your RDS instance:

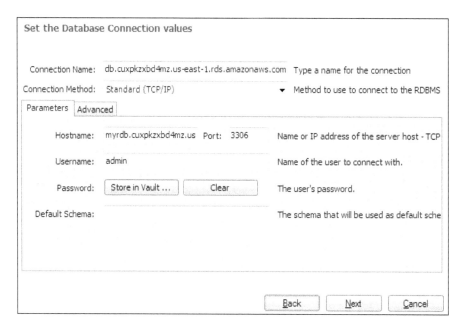

6. Click **Next** and test your database connection:

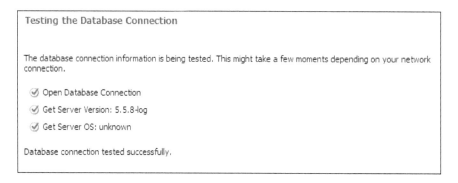

7. Select **Do not use remote management** and proceed past the next dialog.

 Please note that Amazon RDS does not support the management of the MySQL instance supporting RDS directly with MySQL Workbench.

Importing data into the RDS instance

To import data into your RDS instance the options are fairly limited. However, there is a good guide located at:

```
http://aws.amazon.com/articles/2933?_encoding=UTF8
```

The easiest way to import data from your existing MySQL instance is to use **mysqldump** utility and pipe it directly through to **mysql**.

The syntax for this command is:

```
C:\> mysqldump <local MySQL> | mysql --host=<RDS Endpoint> --user=<admin
user> --password=<admin password> <RDS instance name>
```

So for our previous example where the local database is called **test**:

```
C:\> mysqldump test | mysql --host=myrdb.cuxpkzxbd4mz.us-east-1.rds.
amazonaws.com --user=admin --password=222111 myrds
```

Amazon SimpleDB

Amazon **SimpleDB** is a simple key/value data store provided by Amazon for the reliable storage of simple data of any size. While the features of SimpleDB are often too restrictive to replace a relational database, such as SQL Server or Oracle, SimpleDB can often provide value for storing large volumes of simple data that is not required for day-to-day operation of your application. Examples of such data are:

- Logging and access records
- Metadata for objects stored in Amazon S3
- Large volume datasets that require simple index and query functionality

Currently, there are some limitations associated with SimpleDB. These are:

- Each Domain is limited to a total data size of 10 GB
- Currently, the AWS Console does not support SimpleDB

To access SimpleDB, use one of the supplied libraries. Examples of supplied libraries are:

Language	Library Location
.Net	`http://aws.amazon.com/sdkfornet/`
Java	`http://aws.amazon.com/sdkforjava/`
PHP	`http://aws.amazon.com/sdkforphp/`
Ruby	`http://aws.amazon.com/ruby/`

However, for testing, Amazon provides the SimpleDB Scratchpad located at `http://aws.amazon.com/code/1137`.

Getting started with SimpleDB

1. To get started with SimpleDB, browse to `http://aws.amazon.com/simpledb` and click on the **Sign Up for Amazon SimpleDB** button.

2. You will be presented with the now familiar pricing page. Click on **Complete Sign Up** to continue.

3. It will take a few minutes to activate your SimpleDB subscription.

4. Once you have received an e-mail informing that your subscription is active, you will need to install the SimpleDB scratchpad to access and test your SimpleDB functionality.

5. Download the SimpleDB Scratchpad from:

    `http://aws.amazon.com/code/1137`

6. Extract the files from the archive onto your local hard disk, and using your web browser, browse to the local `index.html` file located in the `webapp` directory.

7. The initial page of the application will request that you enter your AWS Access Key ID and your AWS Secret Access Key:

8. Once you have entered your credentials, select the **CreateDomain** in the **Explore API** drop-down combo. This will create the equivalent of a Table.

9. Enter a domain name and select **Invoke Request**:

10. The response will be in RAW XML as follows:

```
<CreateDomainResponse>
<ResponseMetadata>
<RequestId>987ba5cf-ccc5-6acc-517c-66799447405d</RequestId>
<BoxUsage>0.0055590278</BoxUsage>
</ResponseMetadata>
</CreateDomainResponse>
```

11. To add a record to this table in SimpleDB terms, you will need to call the **PutAttributes** API call:

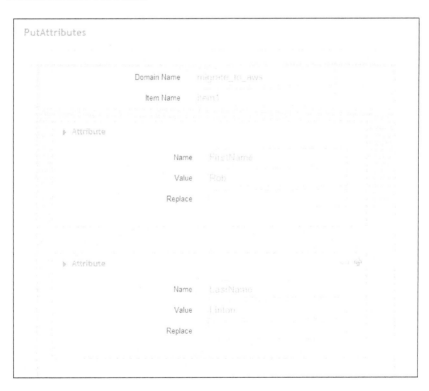

12. The response will also be in raw XML:

```
<PutAttributesResponse>
<ResponseMetadata>
<RequestId>c39bd24f-653d-4fa8-f66b-3ab1d1ade084</RequestId>
<BoxUsage>0.0000219923</BoxUsage>
</ResponseMetadata>
</PutAttributesResponse>
```

13. Now that we have added a 'row' to our 'table' in SQL terms, let's retrieve our record.

14. To retrieve our data, we use the **GetAttributes** API call:

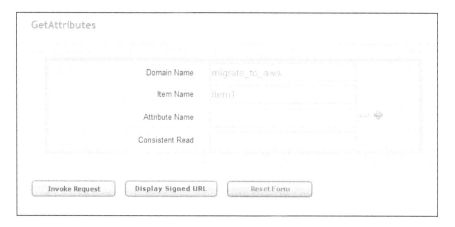

15. The response in raw XML is:

```
<GetAttributesResponse>
<GetAttributesResult>
<Attribute>
<Name>FirstName</Name>
<Value>Rob</Value>
</Attribute>
<Attribute>
<Name>LastName</Name>
<Value>Linton</Value>
</Attribute>
</GetAttributesResult>
<ResponseMetadata>
<RequestId>45643ae7-7e62-1577-2348-f8ad388086cc</RequestId>
<BoxUsage>0.0000093282</BoxUsage>
</ResponseMetadata>
</GetAttributesResponse>
```

16. As can be seen from the previous response, our data is returned in the raw XML.

Downloading the example code

You can download the example code files for all Packt books you have purchased from your account at `http://www.PacktPub.com`. If you purchased this book elsewhere, you can visit `http://www.PacktPub.com/support` and register to have the files e-mailed directly to you.

Any UTF-8 characters that are valid in XML are valid for name, attribute values, or item names.

SimpleDB is useful where there is a need to store simple key/value pairs robustly in the cloud and access them with very short access times (in the order of a few milliseconds). However, it is worthwhile to note that SimpleDB has a 10 GB limit per domain.

For further information on SimpleDB limits please refer to:
`http://docs.amazonwebservices.com/AmazonSimpleDB/latest/DeveloperGuide/SDBLimits.html`.

This completes our brief introduction to SimpleDB.

Summary

In this chapter, we covered in detail how to create both Microsoft SQL Server and Oracle instances on AWS. We looked at how we connect to these instances and how to import data into each of our instances once they were created. We looked at licensing and pricing for both Oracle and SQL Server, and looked at how they were both structured from the AWS cloud perspective.

We also covered Amazon RDS and Amazon SimpleDB, and also gave examples on how to both connect and to import data into these services.

In the next chapter, we bring it all together for our sample application and look at how we configure all of the components and deploy our data and code. We will look at how we manage our application and operationally support it with day-to-day tasks such as performance monitoring and backup of our data.

7
Migrating your Data and Deploying your Code

Well, here we are, finally at the chapter where we will be deploying our sample application up to AWS! In this chapter, we depart from AWS just a little and — just for one chapter — focus on the steps required to make our sample .Net application work. We have spent quite a bit of time so far looking at all of the options that AWS offers; now, in this chapter, we will look in detail at the steps required to deploy our sample application **Waaah (Widgets are always available here)**.

Just to recap: Waaah is a **Microsoft Model View Controller (MVC) 3.0** application, developed with **.Net 4.0** and **Visual Web Developer 2010 Express**. It is a basic web application that allows login/logoff, and subscribe/unsubscribe to a list of services supplied by the **Widget Company**. The database is a SQL Server database, and the application relies on **Forms Security** for authentication. Our application comprises three parts, the web application itself, which runs on the web server; a simple WCF web service that runs on the application servers; and of course the database, of which there are two, one for authentication and one to handle the information on our widgets.

Sample application code

To obtain a copy of the source code for our sample application, please refer to the code bundle on the packtpub site.

To make changes to our sample application, you will need to install Visual Studio 2010 Express, ASP.NET and ASP.NET MVC, and SQL Server Express. Luckily you can do all of these at the same time by visiting: `http://www.asp.net/downloads`

Click on the **Install Now** button and you are away. To load the project, open the `Waaah.sln` file located in the **Waaah** directory. The solution holds both the databases required for the solution to run as well as the required WCF web service:

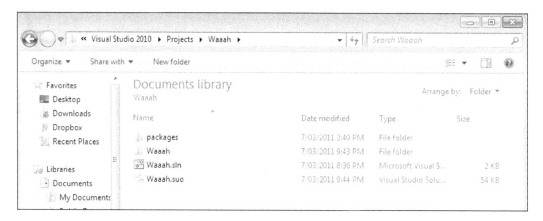

Installing the pre-requisites

In this chapter, we will be installing our software on both the application and web servers, and while we have already done quite a bit of configuration, there is still quite a bit to go. The first thing we will be doing is installing the pre-requisite Microsoft software on both our app and web servers.

Disabling Internet explorer enhanced security configuration

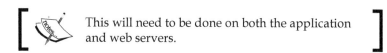

This will need to be done on both the application and web servers.

1. Before we begin, we will need to disable the **Internet Explorer Enhanced Security Configuration (IE ESC)**. To do this, log in to the web server and start the **Programs and Features** application, located in the **Control Panel**:

2. Click on the **Turn Windows features on or off**:

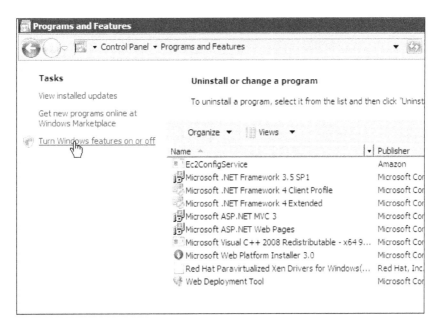

3. This will start the Server Manager console. From within the console select **Configure IE ESC:**

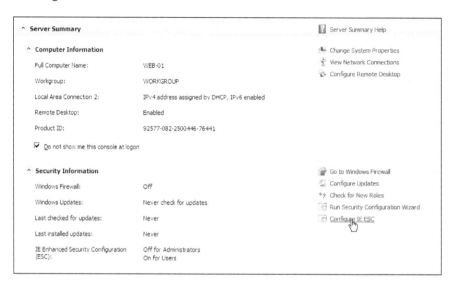

4. Set the option to **Off** for **Administrators**:

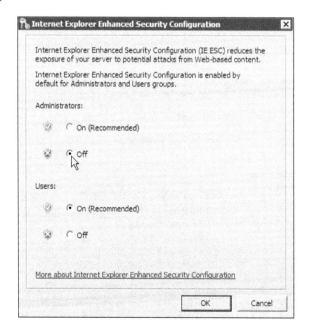

With this disabled, we will now be able to download and install the required software from the Microsoft website.

Installing IIS

 This will need to be done on both the application and web servers.

1. The next step is to install IIS with the application extensions. To do this while still in **Server Manager** click on the **Roles** option and select **Add Roles**:

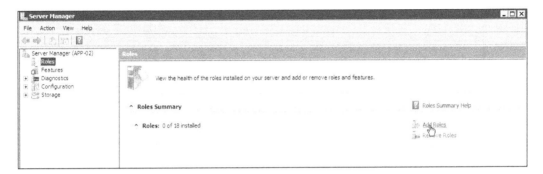

2. You will be presented with the **Add Roles Wizard**:

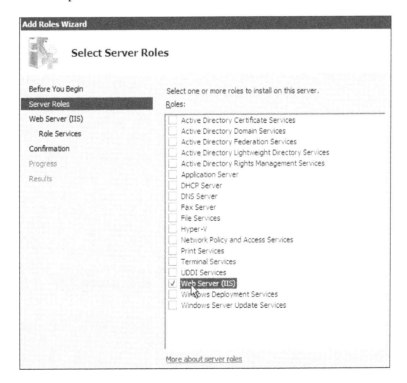

3. Select **Web Server (IIS)** and click **Add Required Features** in the subsequent pop-up dialog:

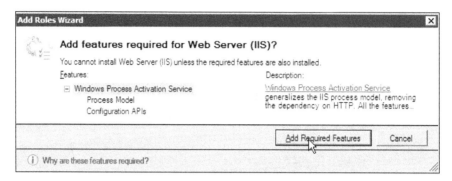

4. Click **Next** on the following information dialog and then select **Application Development** in the **Select Role Services** option:

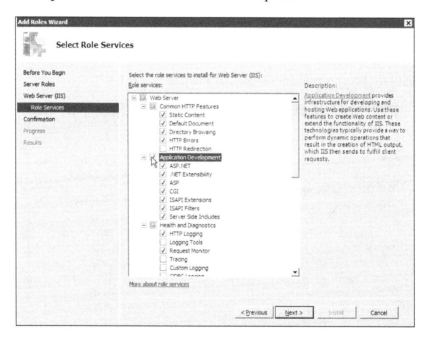

5. You will once again need to accept the **Required Features**. Click **Next** to move on to the following summary screen then click **Install**.

 The install of IIS typically takes around 10 minutes, so you may want to do other things while you wait.

Installing .Net 4.0 and the MVC extensions

 This will need to be done on both the application and web servers.

1. Once IIS is installed, the next step is to install the .Net 4.0 framework as well as the MVC extensions. These are located at:

   `http://www.microsoft.com/web/gallery/install.aspx?appid=MVC3`

2. Click on the **Install** button and follow the prompts:

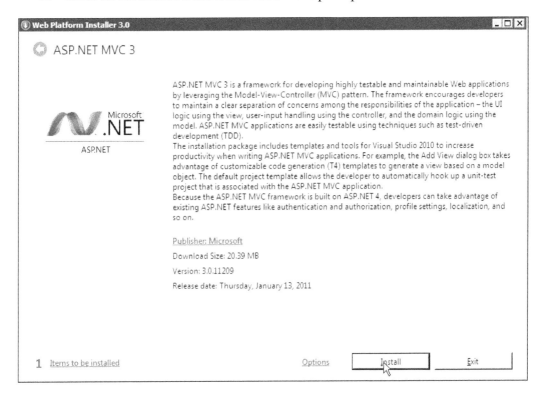

 You will be required to restart each of your servers once ASP.NET MVC3 has been installed.

Configuring IIS

1. Once IIS and MVC have been installed, the next step is to configure IIS.

2. Start the **Internet Information Server (IIS) Manager**, select the server name (in this case **APP-02**) and double-click on the **ISAPI and CGI Restrictions** icon:

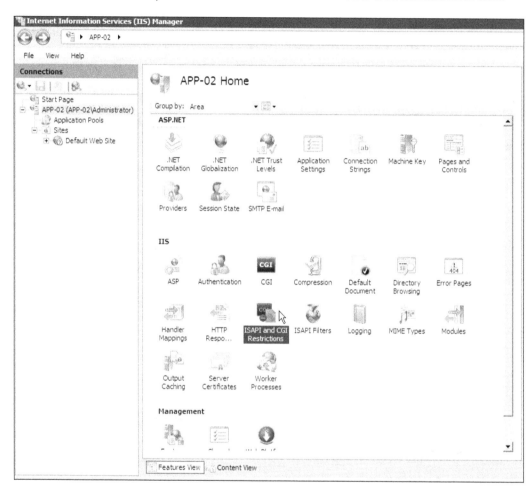

3. In the **ISAPI and CGI Restrictions** option dialog, change the two **ASP.NET v4.0** entries to **Allowed**:

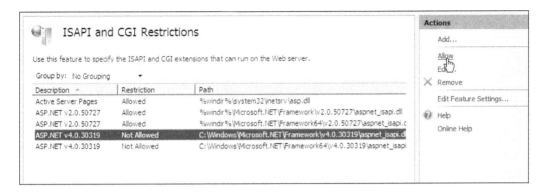

4. While still in **IIS Manager**, select the **Default Web Site** and click on **Advanced Settings**:

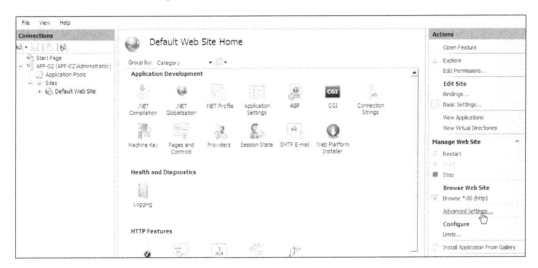

5. Change the **Application Pool** to **ASP.NET v4.0**:

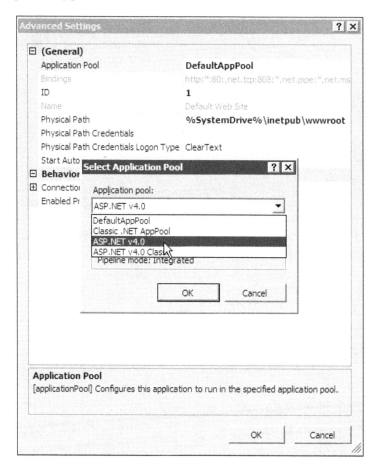

This has completed the initial IIS configuration.

Installing the Application

Now that most of the basics have been completed, it's time to install our application. We will be starting from the database servers and working our way up to the web servers.

Installing the database servers

By default, the version of SQL Server 2008 installed in AWS has no service packs installed.

1. So, as the first step, download and install SQL Server 2008 Service Pack 2 from:

   ```
   http://www.microsoft.com/downloads/en/details.
   aspx?FamilyID=8fbfc1de-d25e-4790-88b5-7dda1f1d4e17
   ```

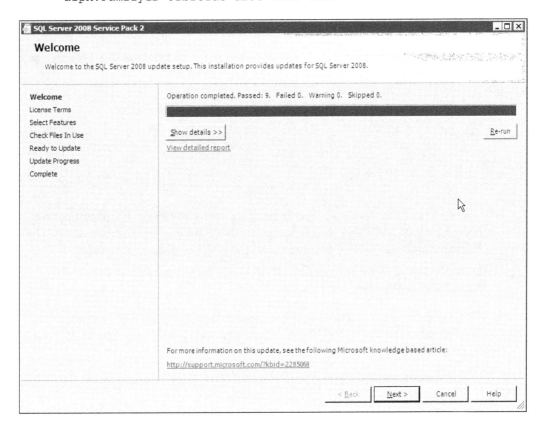

2. Check your firewall settings after SP2 has been installed, as it may make changes that prevent your servers from communicating.

 As part of the Waaah download there are two databases located in the App_Data\2008 database versions directory of our solution. These are versions that can be used with the earlier SQL Server 2008 version of the AMI.

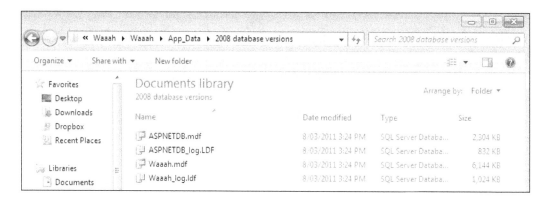

3. The **ASPNETDB** database was created for us by the Forms Authentication framework in ASP.NET and holds all of the login and user information. The **Waaah** database holds information on the services that we provide.

    Copy both of these databases to DB-01 — our first database server — using the techniques learned in our previous chapters.

4. Once you have copied the database file, create three new **EBS Volumes** of 20 GB and attach them to **DB-01**. Name them **SQL-DATA**, **SQL-LOGS**, and **SQL-BACKUP**:

5. Assign them drive letters **F:**, **G:**, and **H:** in line with their device names and initialize and format the drives:

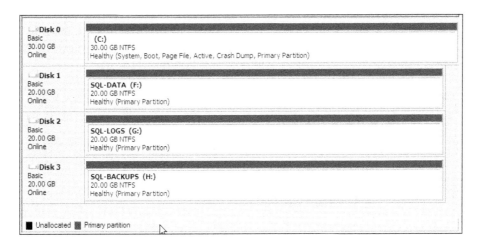

6. Create the following directories:
    - ° `F:\MSSQL\Data`
    - ° `G:\MSSQL\TLogs`
    - ° `H:\MSSQL\Backup`

7. Copy the database `*.MDF` files into `F:\MSSQL\Data` and the `*.LOG` files into `G:\MSSQL\Logs`.

8. Now that the database files have been placed into the correct locations, it's time to attach them to the SQL Server database instance running in this box:

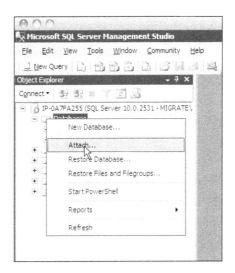

9. Right-click on the **Databases** node in **Microsoft SQL Server Management Studio** and click on **Attach...**.

10. Click on the **Add** button and select each of the *.MDF database files in turn. After adding each one, you will notice that the **Log** file has the message **Not Found** in the **Message** column. Click on the **Current File Path** button and select the correct location for each of the Log files in the G:\ drive:

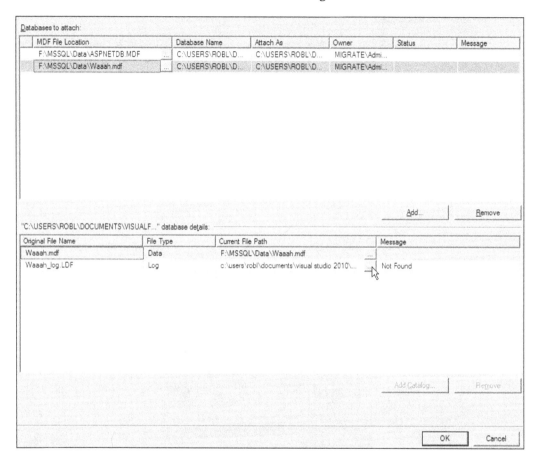

Security

Once you have attached the databases, you will need to create an account for the application to use. In SQL Server Management Studio, click on the **Security | Logins** node and create a local SQL Server account. Grant the account local **dbowner** access to both the Waaah database and the ASPNETDB database.

Mirroring and failover

You may be wondering why we have a second SQL server database server and why both the primary and secondary database servers are part of a domain?

The primary reason is that **SQL Server Mirroring** works much better if both the database servers are part of the same domain. In this sample application, database mirroring has been set up between the two servers. Unfortunately, the process for setting up database mirroring is too complex for this chapter and we have not covered it here.

 If you would like to have a go at setting mirroring up between DB-01 and DB-02, there is a good article at:
`http://msdn.microsoft.com/en-us/library/ms179306.aspx`.

Now that your database files have been attached, we are ready to move up a layer to the application servers.

Application Servers

The application servers will be running our **Windows Communication Foundation (WCF)** service, which is a simple web service that mimics the subscribe/unsubscribe function of our website.

Since we have already done most of the pre-requisites, it is a fairly straightforward matter to install our WCF service.

1. In the Waaah package you downloaded, you will find the folders as shown in the following screenshot:

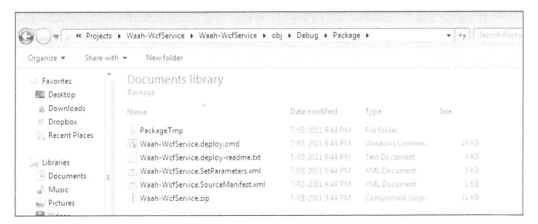

2. Copy all of the files in this directory (but not the `PackageTmp` folder) to a temporary location on the application servers.

3. Open a command prompt and run the following command:

    ```
    C:\Downloads> Waah-WcfService.deploy.cmd /T
    ```

```
Administrator: Command Prompt                                              _ □ X
Microsoft Windows [Version 6.0.6002]
Copyright (c) 2006 Microsoft Corporation.  All rights reserved.

C:\Users\Administrator>cd Downloads

C:\Users\Administrator\Downloads>dir
 Volume in drive C has no label.
 Volume Serial Number is 3EE1-F507

 Directory of C:\Users\Administrator\Downloads

03/08/2011  05:53 AM    <DIR>          .
03/08/2011  05:53 AM    <DIR>          ..
03/08/2011  05:52 AM             3,698 Waah-WcfService.deploy-readme.txt
03/08/2011  05:52 AM            10,193 Waah-WcfService.deploy.cmd
03/08/2011  05:51 AM               163 Waah-WcfService.SetParameters.xml
03/08/2011  05:52 AM               608 Waah-WcfService.SourceManifest.xml
03/08/2011  05:53 AM            10,927 Waah-WcfService.zip
               5 File(s)         25,589 bytes
               2 Dir(s)   7,833,661,440 bytes free

C:\Users\Administrator\Downloads>Waah-WcfService.deploy.cmd /T_
```

4. This will run the install in "test" mode. The first time you install the sample application, you will most likely be prompted to install the following utility:

    ```
    =============================

    Prerequisites :

    ---------------------------

    To deploy this Web package, Web Deploy (msdeploy.exe) must be
    installed on the computer that runs the .cmd file. For information
    about how to install Web Deploy, see the following URL:

    http://go.microsoft.com/?linkid=9278654
    ```

5. Follow the previous link, install the utility, and try again.

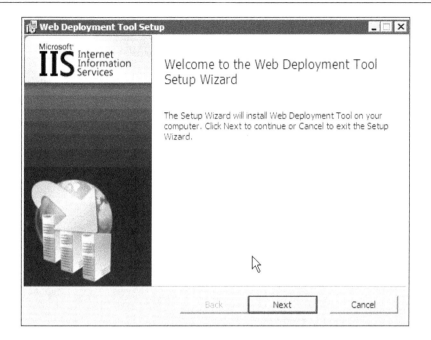

6. This time the test run should work without a hitch. To run the install 'for real', replace the /T with the /Y switch.

   ```
   C:\Downloads> Waah-WcfService.deploy.cmd /Y
   ```

7. To test if the install was successful, browse to the following location: `http://localhost/Waah-WcfService/Widget.svc`.

8. Make sure that the top of the web page looks like the following screenshot:

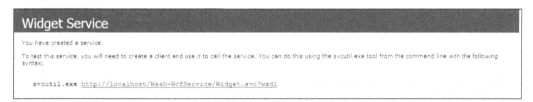

Web Servers

Configuration of the web servers is similar to the configuration of the application servers.

1. Browse to the Waaah install package and copy all of the files (but not the `packageTmp` directory) to each of the web servers from the location, as shown in the following screenshot:

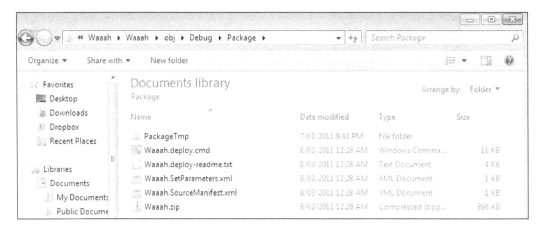

2. Open a command prompt on each web server and run the following command:

   `C:\Downloads> Waaah.deploy.cmd /T`

3. This will test the install, and as before you may need to install the web deployment tool:

```
Administrator: Command Prompt

Microsoft Windows [Version 6.0.6002]
Copyright (c) 2006 Microsoft Corporation.  All rights reserved.

C:\Users\Administrator>cd downloads

C:\Users\Administrator\Downloads>dir
 Volume in drive C has no label.
 Volume Serial Number is 3EE1-F507

 Directory of C:\Users\Administrator\Downloads

03/08/2011  06:17 AM    <DIR>          .
03/08/2011  06:17 AM    <DIR>          ..
03/08/2011  06:16 AM             3,658 Waaah.deploy-readme.txt
03/08/2011  06:17 AM            10,403 Waaah.deploy.cmd
03/08/2011  06:16 AM               541 Waaah.SetParameters.xml
03/08/2011  06:16 AM               548 Waaah.SourceManifest.xml
03/08/2011  06:17 AM           918,757 Waaah.zip
               5 File(s)        933,907 bytes
               2 Dir(s)   7,762,821,120 bytes free

C:\Users\Administrator\Downloads>Waaah.deploy.cmd /T_
```

4. When the tests have passed, run the full command with the /Y option.

    ```
    C:\Downloads> Waaah.deploy.cmd /Y
    ```

5. Once our application code has been installed, the final step is to modify the web.config file on each web server with the new values for where our databases and web services live:

    ○   On the web servers, go to the following directory and edit the web. config file in notepad:

    ```
    C:\inetpub\wwwroot\Waaah\web.config
    ```

    ○   Change the following lines:

    ```
    <connectionStrings>
      <add name="WidgetEntities"
        connectionString="data source=
        ec2-50-16-236-164.compute-1.amazonaws.com;
        User ID=appservice; Password=123456;
        Initial Catalog=Waaah"
        providerName="System.Data.SqlClient"
      />
      <add name="ApplicationServices"
        connectionString="data source=
        ec2-50-16-236-164.compute-1.amazonaws.com;
        User ID=appservice; Password=123456;
        Initial Catalog=ASPNETDB"
        providerName="System.Data.SqlClient"
      />
    </connectionStrings>
    ```

 Please note, the highlighted sections will be different for your own setup.

    ○   At the bottom of the file, change the following line:

    ```
    <client>
      <endpoint
    address="http://ec2-184-73-175-58.compute-1.amazonaws.com/
    Waah-WcfService/Widget.svc"
    binding="basicHttpBinding"
    bindingConfiguration="BasicHttpBinding_IWidget" contract="Wi
    dgetServiceReference.IWidget"
    name="BasicHttpBinding_IWidget"
      />
    </client>
    ```

Note that the application server address will be different for both web servers, as WEB-01 will connect to APP-01 and WEB-02 will connect to APP-02.

Testing our sample application

Now that we have completed the install of our sample application Waaah, let's give it a test run!

Browse to the load balancer address you specified earlier and our sample application should be up and running!

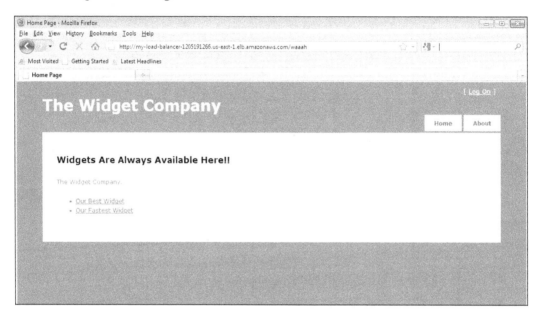

Troubleshooting our application

Hopefully, by the time you get to this section, things are working fine and our sample application Waaah is up and running.

However, if things didn't quite go as planned, here are some basic things to check:

1. Make sure you installed IIS with all of the correct features listed in the previous section.

2. Make sure you have selected ASP.NET v4.0 in IIS as the default .NET runtime.

3. Check and make sure that your `Waaah.deploy.cmd` script did not return any errors.

4. Double-check the modifications made to the `web.config` files, pay special attention to where the quotes are located.

Summary

So, just to recap, in this chapter, we installed our sample application Waaah on AWS. We implemented a load-balanced web server frontend, with each web server connecting to a dedicated application server and to a mirrored database server.

Our sample application was written in Visual Studio 2010 using ASP.NET MVC and the location for the source code for this application as well as instructions on downloading and installing the Microsoft Web Development tools were covered.

At the end of this chapter, we connected to the public address of the AWS load balancer in front of our application and watched it work!

In the next chapter, we will be covering Amazon Simple Queue Service (SQS) and Amazon Simple Notification Service (SNS). We will look at how these technologies can be used in enterprise applications as well as how these services can improve our sample application, Waaah.

8
Amazon's Queuing and Notification Options

As we have seen, Amazon Web Services provides a highly scalable and flexible environment for running enterprise applications. In the previous chapters, we have looked at migrating our existing applications pretty much unaltered to AWS. However, in this chapter, we will look at two new technologies provided by AWS that we can use to enhance our existing enterprise application.

The first of these is **Simple Queue Service (SQS)** and the second service we will be looking at is **Simple Notification Service (SNS)**.

Simple Queue Service (SQS)

SQS is a messaging system designed to allow distributed components to communicate and share work in a loosely coupled manner. SQS allows jobs to be created in one part of the system, and then consumed in another. At this time, there is no web interface to SQS provided in the AWS Console, so we will be using the SQS scratchpad provided by Amazon as well as Visual Web Developer 2010 Express to run samples provided by Amazon.

Getting started

To get started with SQS, we will need to download and install a couple of tools, **SQS Scratchpad** and the **AWS SDK for .Net** and sample code.

SQS Scratchpad

1. The first tool we will be downloading is the SQS scratchpad. The **SQS scratchpad** is a simple locally run web application that allows simple calls to be made to the SQS service. To download the scratchpad, browse to:

   `http://aws.amazon.com/code/1254`

2. Download the zip file to your previously created `C:\AWS` directory and create a directory called `C:\AWS\SQS`.

3. Unzip the file and drill down until you get to the `webapp` directory and copy this to your newly created `C:\AWS\SQS` directory.

4. To run the scratchpad, double-click on the `C:\AWS\SQS\webapp\index.html` file and open it in your browser. The following screen should be presented if all goes well.

AWS SDK for .Net library and sample code

1. The AWS .Net libraries contain code and examples for the majority of Amazon Web Services in one package. To install the package, browse to:

   `http://aws.amazon.com/sdkfornet/`

   You should see the following page:

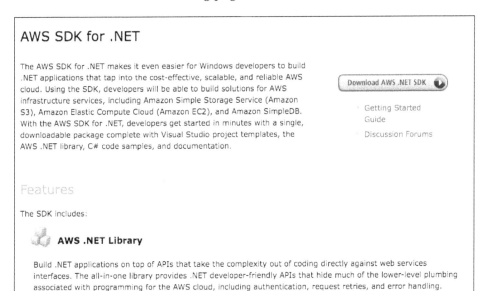

2. Install the **Software Development Kit (SDK)** by running the setup file and follow the prompts.

3. Once the SDK has been installed, the first thing you will need to do is copy the sample C# solution from the following directory `C:\Program Files\AWS SDK for .NET\Samples\AmazonSQS_Sample` to a new directory located at `C:\AWS\SQS\AmazonSQS_Sample`.

 Under the 64-bit version of Windows Vista or Windows 7, the path is slightly different: **C:\Program Files(x86)\ AWS SDK for .NET\Samples**

4. After you have copied it to its new location, start **Microsoft Visual Web Developer 2010 Express** and open the solution file located at `C:\AWS\SQS\AmazonSQS_Sample\AmazonSQS_Sample.sln`.

Since the file was created in an earlier version of Visual Studio, you will be prompted to convert the project; select **Yes** and allow visual Studio to convert it. Once the project has been loaded up, you will need to enter your Access Key and your Secret Access Key. To do that open the **App.config** file and add the values for both your **AWSAccessKey** and **AWSSecretKey**.

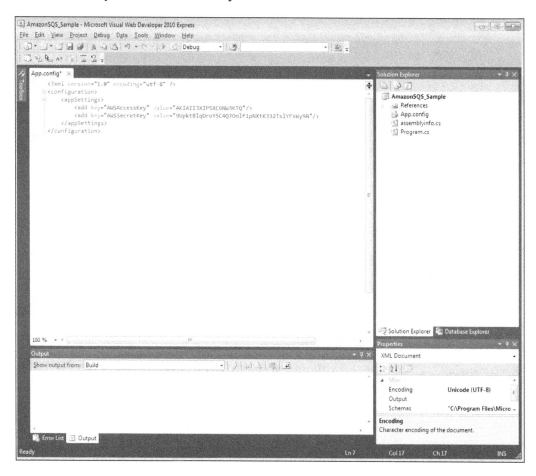

We are now ready to start with SQS!

An overview of how SQS works

To show how SQS works, let's illustrate it in the following diagrams:

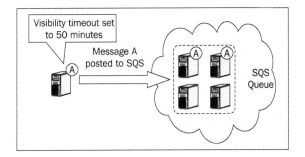

In the first diagram, a message is posted to an SQS queue; notice that the message does not exist on all of the SQS messaging servers. This is important to note, a "get" from a queue may return nothing even when there are messages still waiting; however, multiple 'gets' will be guaranteed to obtain all messages eventually. Also note that when a message is posted to an SQS queue, a **Visibility Timeout** is specified. This sets the maximum amount of time a message may be processed for. Once a message has passed this timeout, it is available for processing again by other service consumers.

 All messages do not exist on all servers in SQS, so multiple SQS 'gets' may be required to get all messages.

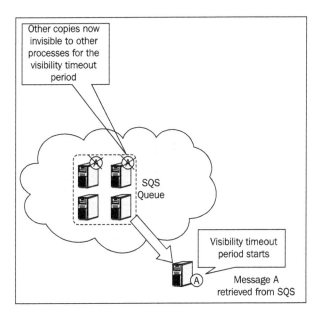

In the second diagram, Message A is retrieved from the queue and the visibility timer starts. All other instances of the message are now invisible to other components retrieving messages from the queue for the visibility timeout period.

 Remember to delete the message after you have processed it or it will become visible again after the visibility timeout period has expired.

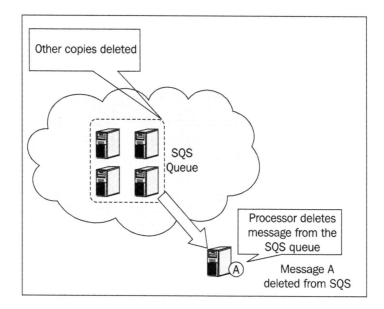

In the final diagram, Message A is deleted from the SQS Queue.

 If messages are not deleted, they are removed from the queue automatically after four days.

Creating your first queue

To create your first queue start the SQS Scratchpad and enter your Access Key and Secret Access Key in the fields at the top. Then select **CreateQueue** from the **Explore API:** drop-down combo.

Enter an SQS queue name and a default visibility timeout and click on the **Invoke Request** button. An XML response will be returned in XML format as follows, with the URL of the queue returned in the **QueueUrl** field.

```
<CreateQueueResponse>
  <CreateQueueResult>
    <QueueUrl>
      https://queue.amazonaws.com/764516644405/migrate_to_aws_queue
    </QueueUrl>
  </CreateQueueResult>
  <ResponseMetadata>
    <RequestId>9a0b110a-8cb3-4c1b-98b5-32811b19062f</RequestId>
  </ResponseMetadata>
</CreateQueueResponse>
```

To confirm that the queue exists, select the **ListQueues** option from the **ExploreAPI** drop-down combo and click on the **Invoke Request** button. In the XML returned, you should see your queue listed after a short while.

 It may take a couple of seconds for your new queue to be created and propagated throughout the SQS system.

Testing the full SQS lifecycle of a message

Now to test the full lifecycle of SQS, open up the **AmazonSQS_Sample** in **Microsoft Visual Web Developer 2010 Express** and click on **Debug | Start Debugging** menu item, or press *F5*. This example program illustrates all of the steps of using SQS; the following screenshot is the output:

If you would like to look at the code used to implement these steps, open up the `Program.cs` file listed in the **Solution Explorer**.

In this example, the steps are:

1. Create a queue called MyQueue.
2. Confirm that the queue exists by printing a list of existing queues.
3. Send a message to MyQueue.
4. Receive a message from MyQueue.
5. Print the received message.
6. Delete the message from MyQueue.

SQS pricing and limits

Currently the pricing of SQS is $0.000001 per request, with the first 1 GB of data per month free.

A single queue may contain an unlimited number of messages, and you can create an unlimited number of queues.

Simple Notification Service (SNS)

Simple Notification Service (SNS) is a real-time messaging service designed to allow applications to send alerts and messages to multiple receivers at the same time. Amazon has kindly provided a tab for us to manage our SNS subscriptions in the AWS Console, so we will be using this to manage our SNS service. Also, we will be using an external service called `www.postbin.org`, an excellent website used for visualising **Web Hooks** used by services such as SNS.

An overview of how SNS works

SNS works by providing a **Topic**, which can be **Subscribed** to by multiple subscribers using various technologies, such as e-mail and HTTP. By providing a single topic, one message, when posted, may be reliably delivered to multiple subscribers. An example of this is an alert, which may be posted by an application such as our Waaah sample application.

 Later on in this chapter, I will show how we can modify Waaah to make use of both SQS and SNS to enhance its existing functionality.

Getting started

To get started with SNS, you will need to sign up for the service in the AWS console. Once you have signed up for SNS, clicking on the SNS tab at the top of the AWS console will bring you to the SNS overview.

As you can see, the first thing we will need to do is to create a topic. You can do this by clicking on the **Create New Topic** button as shown in the previous screenshot. Click on the button and enter a name for your new topic. Once it has been created, the AWS Console will display the topic name in the **Navigation** window on the left-hand side of the AWS Console. Clicking on this will show the topic details. Every topic will have an ARN associated with it, which is used by AWS to uniquely identify it.

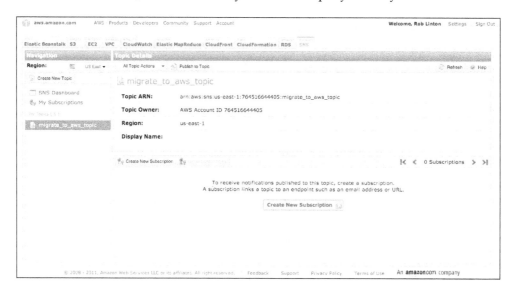

Creating a subscription

Once your topic has been created, let's go ahead and create a Subscription to it. We are going to create two subscriptions to our new topic, an e-mail subscription, and a HTTP subscription. Firstly, let's create an e-mail subscription.

Creating an e-mail subscription

To create an e-mail subscription, click on the **Create New Subscription** button and select **Email**.

Once you have entered in a valid e-mail address, click on the **Subscribe** button. As soon as you do this, the following message will be displayed:

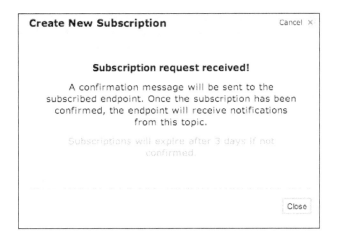

This is an important point to note. The recipient *must* confirm all subscriptions to a topic. When the subscription type is **Email**, the confirmation process is for AWS to send an initial e-mail to the subscription's e-mail address. Clicking on the supplied link in the e-mail will confirm the subscription.

If you look at the topic in the AWS Console, you will note that the subscription is **Pending Confirmation** at this point.

The e-mail will look something like the following screenshot (depending on your e-mail system):

Clicking on the **Confirm subscription** link will confirm the subscription in AWS and show the following response:

If we now look at the AWS console, we can see that the status of the subscription is now confirmed with a **Subscription ID** now populated:

Testing our SNS subscription

Now that we have a valid subscription to our topic, the **Publish to Topic** button is enabled. Click on the button and enter in a **Subject** and a **Message** and click on the **Publish Message** button.

The following message should arrive in your inbox:

Note the unsubscribe options, even with application notifications you should always enable an unsubscribe option; luckily SNS takes care of this for us.

Testing a HTTP subscription

1. Now let's add another subscription, but this time an HTTP one. You may be wondering just how an HTTP subscription works? Well, a HTTP subscription is essentially a POST from SNS to a URL that you provide as your endpoint.

2. To test an HTTP subscription, we are going to use the website `www.postbin.org`. We will be able to create an HTTP endpoint at postbin, which we will then add to SNS. So, to start, browse to `www.postbin.org` and click on the **Make a PostBin** button.

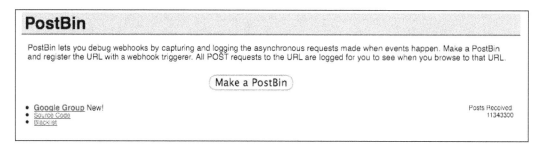

3. This will return a postbin URL in your address bar:

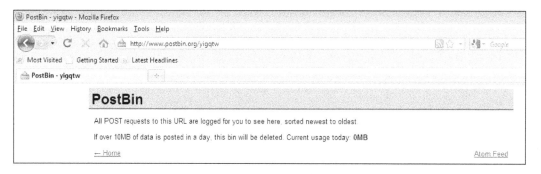

4. In the SNS AWS Console, select our topic and click on the **Create Subscription** button again, but this time select HTTP and cut and paste the postbin URL from `www.postbin.org` into the endpoint box. In our following example, the postbin was:

```
http://www.postbin.org/yigqtw
```

5. Once again a subscription confirmation will be initially posted to the endpoint. To confirm the new HTTP endpoint, browse to your postbin address, you will see the confirmation message listed as the only message.

PostBin

All POST requests to this URL are logged for you to see here, sorted newest to oldest.

#kgbw30 @ 02:42 Mar 25 2011 -- 72.21.217.96   Content | Headers

```
body {
        "Message": "You have chosen to subscribe to the topic arn:aws:sns:us-east-1:764516644405:migra
        "MessageId": "1f5b9523-dfd1-49a0-97fa-1f734a2a09ff",
        "Signature": "NwyEGejmeju2z7Krua-2Dln3v1jLirpVGNw\/b9e8gL31CFYQ\/e5AiL7YGwnIaVi801hYi2LKEdMSQ5
        "SignatureVersion": "1",
        "SigningCertURL": "https:\/\/sns.us-east-1.amazonaws.com\/SimpleNotificationService-f3ecfb7224
        "SubscribeURL": "https:\/\/sns.us-east-1.amazonaws.com\/?Action=ConfirmSubscription&TopicArn=a
        "Timestamp": "2011-03-25T02:42:00.660Z",
        "Token": "2336412f37fb687f5d51e6e241d3b4d5c22816d65c95996ce574e23f964c1c36262653da4d55dd47bbba
        "TopicArn": "arn:aws:sns:us-east-1:764516644405:migrate_to_aws_topic",
        "Type": "SubscriptionConfirmation"
    }
```

If over 10MB of data is posted in a day, this bin will be deleted. Current usage today: 0MB

← Home   Atom Feed

6. To confirm the subscription, cut and paste the **SubscribeURL** into the address bar of your browser, edit it as described next, and then press *Enter*.

7. You will need to edit the URL in two places by removing the "\"'s, highlighted as follows:

```
https:\/\/sns.us-east-1.amazonaws.com\/?Action=ConfirmSubscriptio
n &TopicArn=arn:aws:sns:us-east-1:764516644405:migrate_to_aws_to
pic&Token=2336412f37fb687f5d51e6e241d3b4d5c22816d65c95996ce574e2
3f964c1c36262653da4d55dd47bbba36dde6f045c1a2d5384d328c4efc66098
5fcd44efa19d 76334b4cd723ac97140471b3f9b1cfa9bc4b3c9dcf583e6fe7
f5cbb5aec6957b071bbd56f4d811be9c1608321bf46400fc3b0d029b03777b2886
454984d5d80
```

8. This will return an XML document showing that the subscription is confirmed.

9. Now post another message to your topic, this time you will receive two copies of the message from SNS, one sent to your e-mail account, and one sent to the HTTP endpoint on `postbin.org`.

Please note, only messages posted to a topic after a subscription is created will be posted to that subscription, previous messages will be ignored.

SNS pricing and limits

Currently the pricing of SQS is free. However, there is a cost for each subsequent block of 100,000 HTTP requests of $0.06, with the first 1 GB of data per month free.

There is currently a limit of 100 SNS topics per AWS account.

Applying SQS and SNS to our sample application

Now that we have an understanding of both SQS and SNS, let's see how we can apply them to our sample application Waaah. If we look back at the previous chapter, we saw that our sample application was composed of three parts, an SQL Server Database, a WCF Web Service for subscribing and unsubscribing to widgets, and a MVC web application.

In our current architecture, there is only one way to subscribe/unsubscribe to widgets for our Widget Company, and that is through our MVC Web application, Waaah.

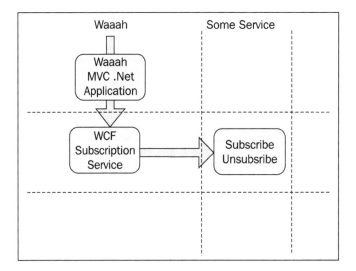

While this was the initial design choice for this application, wouldn't it be great if—now that we have migrated our sample application to AWS—we could open up the Subscribe/Unsubscribe service to other applications. So let's look at how we would integrate these two services into our sample application Waaah.

Firstly, let's decouple the **WCF Subscription Service** from our **Subscribe/Unsubscribe** service by placing **SQS** between them. Then let's add another access channel by hooking up **SNS** to our **SQS** service.

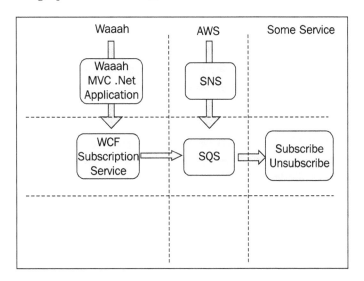

As you can see from the previous diagram, instead of only being able to subscribe to widgets via our web application, we can now subscribe/unsubscribe from other AWS applications by submitting requests to SQS, or we can even subscribe by sending an SNS notification to the appropriate SNS topic.

In the previous example, we would create a new SQS queue called Waaah_Queue. We would then create a new SNS Topic called Waaah_Topic, which we would then create a subscription to using the SQS endpoint of the queue we just created in SQS. We could even create another e-mail subscription to our Waaah_Topic so that we are notified every time someone creates a subscribe/unsubscribe request via the SNS service. All of this is handled transparently by AWS with minimal requirement. In fact, the only change to our WCF Service was the addition of less than ten lines of code, allowing the WCF Service to send a message to our SQS queue every time it was called.

Because the examples provided do not contain an example of how to implement SNS, I have included a sample for you here:

```
AmazonSimpleNotificationService sns =
  AWSClientFactory.CreateAmazonSNSClient(key, secret);

PublishRequest req = new PublishRequest();
req.WithMessage("This is my test message");
req.WithSubject("The Test Subject");
req.WithTopicArn(topicArn);
PublishResponse result = sns.Publish(req);
```

Summary

In this chapter, we looked at the Amazon Simple Queue Service (SQS) and the Amazon Simple Notification Service (SNS). We looked at how we use these AWS services and walked through implementing and using these services step by step. When we had finished looking at both of these services, we looked at how we could implement these services to enhance our sample application Waaah.

In the next chapter, we will be looking at how to monitor our application now that it is up on AWS as well as how to scale our application using some of the services we have already looked at in AWS.

9
Monitoring and Scaling My Application

In the last chapter, we looked at how we could use Amazon's queuing and notification services to add value to our existing application. We looked at how we could use these services to open up our application to other services running in our AWS environment.

In this chapter, we will be looking at how monitoring and autoscaling can be added to make our application nimble enough to withstand unexpected failures and spikes in traffic. As part of this, we will be looking at:

- Amazon CloudWatch
- Autoscaling

Autoscaling

Autoscaling is a feature of AWS that allows extra EC2 instances to be added to your infrastructure automatically during periods of high load, and then allows the same instances to be decommissioned automatically when the load has passed. While this seems great in principle, in practice, this is harder to achieve than the hype suggests.

One of the biggest hurdles to overcome that enable Autoscaling to be practical is that most enterprise applications are not built around the principles of scaling horizontally. Let's take a look at our sample enterprise application Waaah:

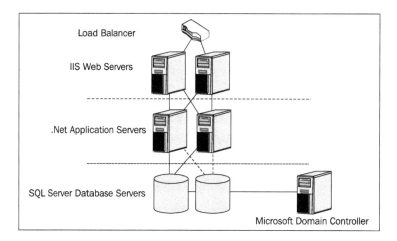

As seen in the previous diagram, while both the web servers and the application servers can scale horizontally, the database servers are limited to one instance. Using Microsoft SQL Server, we can provide redundancy and failover as in the case of the architecture previously mentioned, but we cannot add extra SQL Server instances and expect the load to be evenly balanced between them.

For example, if the load on our sample application Waaah doubled, we could double the number of web servers and application servers as follows:

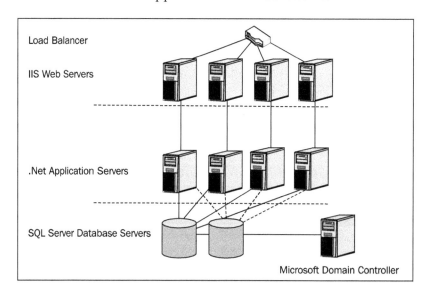

But we couldn't double the number of database servers.

However, this is a good start. Amazon web services provide autoscaling—that we can use to manage the web and application servers—which we will look at implementing in the following sections.

Installing the AWS Autoscaling tools

1. To get started with **AWS Autoscaling**, we will need to install the autoscaling command-line tools and the **CloudWatch** command-line tools, as autoscaling has yet to be implemented into the AWS console. To install the tools, go to the following URL and download the **Auto Scaling API Tools**:

    `http://aws.amazon.com/developertools/2535`

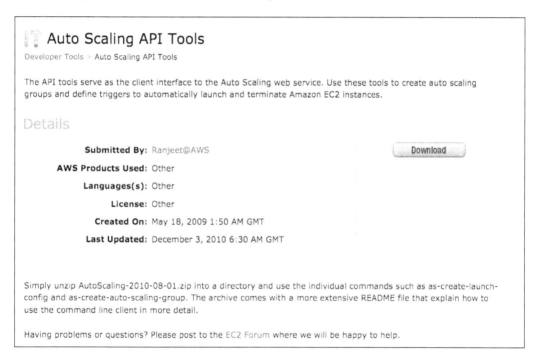

2. Extract the ZIP file and copy the `Autoscaling-1.0.33.1` directory to your previously located `C:\AWS` location.

 You may find that the version is slightly different as the tools are regularly updated.

3. Now edit the `aws_env.cmd` file that we created earlier and add the following two lines:

```
set AWS_AUTO_SCALING_HOME=C:\AWS\AutoScaling-1.0.33.1

set PATH=C:\AWS\AutoScaling-1.0.33.1\bin;%PATH%
```

4. To run the tools firstly change to the `C:\AWS` directory and run the `aws_env.cmd` file. All of the tools should now be available.

5. To test if everything is working correctly, run the following command:

```
C:\AWS> as-describe-launch-configs
```

You should see the following output, as at this point we haven't set up our Autoscaling:

```
C:\Windows\system32\cmd.exe

c:\AWS>aws_env.cmd

c:\AWS>as-describe-launch-configs
No launch configurations found

c:\AWS>
```

Installing the CloudWatch API tools

1. To install the Amazon CloudWatch tools, go to the following URL:

   `http://aws.amazon.com/developertools/2534`

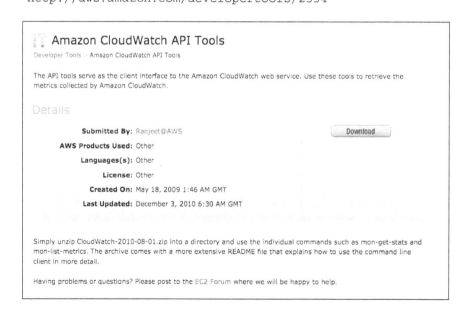

2. Extract the ZIP file and copy the `CloudWatch-1.0.9.5` directory to your previously located `C:\AWS` location.

> You may find that the version is slightly different as the tools are regularly updated.

3. Now edit the previously created `aws_env.cmd` file and add the following two lines:

```
set AWS_CLOUDWATCH_HOME=C:\AWS\CloudWatch-1.0.9.5
set PATH=C:\AWS\CloudWatch-1.0.9.5\bin;%PATH%
```

4. To run the tools firstly change to the `C:\AWS` directory and run the `aws_env.cmd` file. All of the tools should now be available.

5. To test if everything is working correctly, run the following command:

```
C:\AWS> mon-describe-alarms
```

You should see the following output, as at this point we haven't set up any alarms:

Architecture changes to Waaah for autoscaling

Now that we have installed our autoscaling tools, let's look at how we implement autoscaling. The first thing to understand about autoscaling is that it doesn't understand anything about our architecture or how we connect between servers. Autoscaling will look at a set of conditions and based on the result either start up or shutdown a new EC2 instance based on an EC2 image that we supply. So immediately we can see that any servers that we autoscale must be able to be set up exactly the same.

If we look at the architecture shown previously, we can see that this isn't currently the case, each web server connects to the corresponding application server located below it, that requires a connection string change to each web server. To remedy this, we will be introducing another AWS load balancer between the web server layer and the application server layer as follows:

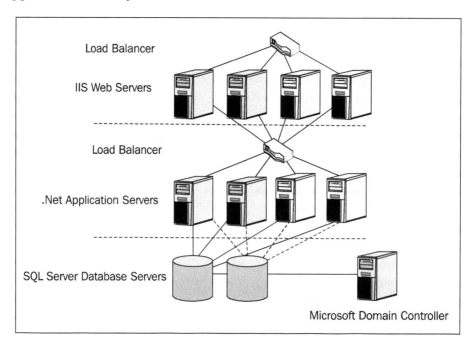

Then we will modify the connection string for the application server in our web servers to point to the **AWS Load Balancer**. One of the added benefits of this is that we no longer need to allocate **Elastic IP Addresses** to each app server, as the load balancer address will be the only address we need.

Creating the application server load balancer

So to get started let's create an application server load balancer. In the AWS console, select **Load Balancers** in the left-hand navigation pane and click on the **Create Load Balancer** button. Give it a name and remove the **Apache HTTP Server** entry and add a **Microsoft IIS** entry instead. Click on **Continue** and edit the Ping path to the address of your WCF application service. In our case, it is `/Waah-WcfService/Widget.svc`. Click on **Continue** and add the current two application server instances.

An important note to make is that AWS load balancers cannot use AWS security groups and therefore cannot currently be secured. At this point in time, the only way around is to use your own load balancer rather than the AWS load balancer for the middle tier. A good example of an alternative to ELB is **HAProxy** (http://haproxy.1wt.eu).

Creating the autoscaling configuration

Now that we have completed the changes necessary to our web and application servers, it's time to start configuring our autoscaling configuration. In our configuration, we will allow the number of web servers and application servers to double when the load increases, and then decrease to the original size when the load decreases.

To make this happen, the first thing we need to do is specify the **Amazon Machine Image (AMI)** and an **EC2 Instance Type**. We do that in a launch configuration.

After we have created our launch configuration (so we know what machine image to launch on what instance type), we need to specify the **Auto Scaling Group**. The autoscaling group defines which availability zone your instances will spin up in and defines the minimum and maximum number of instances that are allowed to operate.

Once these have been created, we will then need to define our scale-up and our scale-down policies, and link them to a **CloudWatch** metric.

Creating the launch configuration

To create the launch configuration, first we need to create an AMI. The easiest way to do this is to take a copy of one of our existing web servers and application servers using the **Create Image (EBS AMI)** command in the **Instances** window in the AWS console.

Once you have created your AMIs, run the following command:

```
C:\AWS> as-create-launch-config <NAME> --image-id <AMI> --instance-type
<INSTANCE TYPE> --group <SECURITY GROUP>
```

For example, if your AMI was called `ami-7cb54915` and the instance type was `m1.large`, then the command would be:

```
C:\AWS> as-create-launch-config WebLaunchConfig --image-id ami-7cb54915
--instance-type m1.large –group "Web Servers"
```

Where the name of the launch configuration would be `WebLaunchConfig`.

Note the –group option, this makes sure that any new instances are launched into the correct security group when they are launched.

This will create a launch configuration for our web servers. Repeat this for the application server, so that we have a launch group for both the web and application servers.

Creating the autoscaling group

Now that we have created our launch configurations, we need to create autoscaling groups for both the web servers and the application servers. When we create the group, we will be able to specify the load balancer that the group will service. To do this run the following command:

```
C:\AWS> as-create-auto-scaling-group WebAutoScaleGroup --launch-
configuration WebLaunchConfig --availability-zones us-east-1a --min-size
2 --max-size 4 -load-balancers my-load-balancer
```

This will set both the availability zone as well as the maximum and minimum number of instances in our group.

After creating your autoscale groups, go to the AWS console and take a look at the running instances. The first thing you will see is two more instances based on your web servers and two more instances based on your application servers running. As soon as you created the autoscale groups they became active!

 It will take a couple of minutes after creating the autoscale group before the group starts up the minimum two instances.

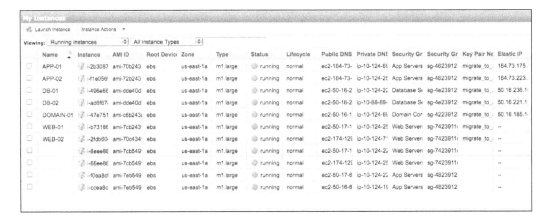

Let's take a moment to look at the previous screenshot. As you can see, after creating an autoscale group for both our web servers and application servers, four new instances have been created. Two of these instances are in the **App Servers** security group, and two are in the **Web Servers** security group. Note, however, that they are not named, nor do they have an associated key pair.

 We could have specified the key pair when we specified the launch config by using the -key option.

Now let's take a look at our load balancers:

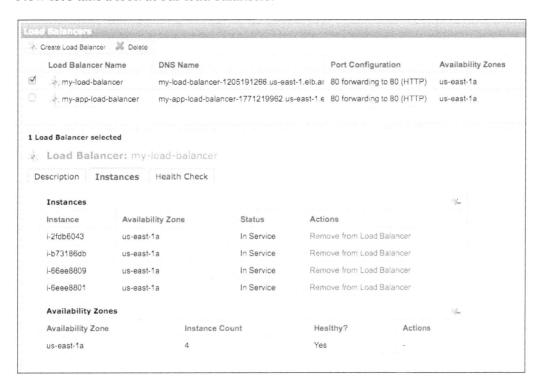

As we can see from the previous screenshot, we have two more instances that have been added to our web load balancer automatically. We know that they are operating correctly because the status for all four of the instances (the two original instances and the two new instances) is all **In Service**.

However, our autoscaling group, at this point, does not respond to changes in the load on our web servers and our applications servers. To enable this, first we will need to create a **Policy** and then link it to a CloudWatch metric.

Creating an autoscale policy

The autoscale policy can be thought of as the action that will occur when an event in the CloudWatch gets triggered. We will need to create two policies, one to scale up, and one to scale down.

To create our scale-up policy, first we will need to make a few decisions. We will need to decide on whether we will adjust the size of our autoscale pool of servers to a fixed amount, by a percentage or by a number. We will also need to decide on how long we wait between autoscaling events. For example, if we decide to add another server, how long do we wait until we add another server if the load is still high.

For our sample application Waaah, we are going to add one server at a time and we are going to wait 2 minutes or 120 seconds between autoscaling events. To create the scale-up policy run the following command:

```
C:\AWS> as-put-scaling-policy WebScaleUp --type ChangeInCapacity
--adjustment 1 --cooldown 120 --auto-scaling-group WebAutoScaleGroup
```

This will return the **Amazon Resource Name** (**ARN**) of the scaling policy.

Run the same command again to create the scale-down policy, but this time change the adjustment to `-1` and the name to `WebScaleDown`:

```
C:\AWS> as-put-scaling-policy WebScaleDown --type ChangeInCapacity
"--adjustment=-1" --cooldown 120 --auto-scaling-group WebAutoScaleGroup
```

 Note the use of quotes and the equals sign when specifying negative values.

Creating the CloudWatch metric

Now that we have created our autoscaling policy, we need to hook them up to a CloudWatch metric. To do this, we need the following information:

- The name of the metric
- The period
- The threshold

For our sample application Waaah, we'll use the following rule:

> *"If the average CPU over a period of 30 seconds is above 80 percent, then call the WebScaleUp policy"*

To implement this, run the following command:

```
C:\AWS> mon-put-metric-alarm WebHighCPUAlarm --comparison-
operator GreaterThanThreshold --evaluation-periods 1 --metric-name
CPUUtilization --namespace "AWS/EC2" --period 120 --statistic
Average --threshold 80 --alarm-actions arn:aws:autoscaling:us-east-
1:764516644405:scalingPolicy:d3c53ac8-fa73-4cfd-9a06-a5f9d7e1a58f:autoSca
lingGroupName/WebAutoScaleGroup:policyName/WebScaleUp --dimensions "AutoS
calingGroupName=WebAutoScaleGroup"
```

In the previous screenshot, you can see both the commands for adding a scale-up metric as well as a scale-down metric.

There is quite a bit to this command, so let's break it down into its individual components:

Command	Description
--comparison-operator GreaterThanThreshold	This defines whether the metric is a greater than or less than threshold. Typically, this would be GreaterThanThreshold for a scale-up metric, and a LessThanThreshold for a scale-down metric.
--evaluation-periods 1	This defines the number of consecutive periods that the value needs to be compared to before action is taken.
--metric-name CPUUtilization	This is the name of the metric to measure. There are many metrics to choose from within the CloudWatch API, to get a list of them run the mon-list-metrics command.
--namespace "AWS/EC2"	This is the namespace of the metric. The value should always be set to the above for autoscaling.
--period 120	This is the period over which the metric should be compared.

Command	Description
`--statistic Average`	This is the metric value to use.
`--threshold 80`	The threshold is measured in percent for this metric. For the alarm to be triggered, in this case, the Average CPU over a period of 120 seconds must be over 80 percent.
`--alarm-actions arn:aws:autoscaling:us-east-1:764516644405:scalingPolicy: d3c53ac8-fa73-4cfd-9a06-a5f9d 7e1a58f:autoScalingGroupName/ WebAutoScaleGroup:policyName/ WebScaleUp`	This is the ARN that was created when the policy was created.
`--dimensions "AutoScalingGroup Name=WebAutoScaleGroup"`	This limits the scope of what servers to monitor, in this case, just monitor the servers, which are part of the autoscaling group WebAutoScaleGroup.

Checking our autoscaling

Now that we have attached our policies to our CloudWatch alarms, our autoscaling configuration is complete.

To check the status of our alarms, run the following command:

`C:\AWS>mon-describe-alarms`

Looking at the output from the previous command, we can see that the WebHighCPUAlarm is currently in an OK status, which makes sense in this situation, as there are currently no users using our sample application Waaah. The WebLowCPUAlarm, however, shows a status of ALARM, which also makes sense, as the CPU average was sitting on zero when this screenshot was taken.

Each time the ALARM is triggered, an instance will be added, or an instance will be taken away, up to the minimum and maximum limits set for the autoscale group—in this case the minimum was two and the maximum was four.

To get a summary of our autoscale group, run the following command:

```
C:\AWS> as-describe-auto-scaling-groups --headers
```

This will return the following:

```
C:\Windows\system32\cmd.exe
c:\AWS>as-describe-auto-scaling-groups
AUTO-SCALING-GROUP  AppAutoScaleGroup  AppLaunchConfig  us-east-1a  my-app-load-balancer  2  4  2
INSTANCE  i-f0ea8c9f  us-east-1a  InService  Healthy  AppLaunchConfig
INSTANCE  i-ccea8ca3  us-east-1a  InService  Healthy  AppLaunchConfig
AUTO-SCALING-GROUP  WebAutoScaleGroup  WebLaunchConfig  us-east-1a  my-load-balancer  2  4  2
INSTANCE  i-6eee8801  us-east-1a  InService  Healthy  WebLaunchConfig
INSTANCE  i-66ee8809  us-east-1a  InService  Healthy  WebLaunchConfig
c:\AWS>
```

Final configuration changes

Now that our autoscaling is complete for both our web servers and our application servers, we can stop our initial web servers (WEB01 and WEB02) and our initial application servers (APP01 and APP02) as these servers are no longer required. After these servers have been shut down, we can release the elastic IP addresses back to AWS for the application servers, as these are no longer required.

We have now completed our implementation of autoscaling on AWS. Here is our final architecture:

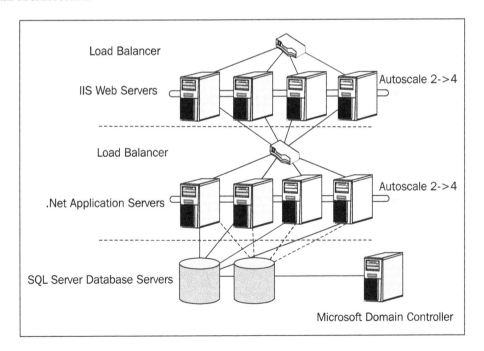

Pricing for autoscaling

There is no cost for implementing autoscaling in AWS other than the cost of the EC2 instances themselves when they are started.

Using Amazon CloudWatch to monitor our application

In the previous sections, we briefly looked at how we can use **Amazon CloudWatch** to monitor and trigger alarms for use in autoscaling. In this section, we will look at how CloudWatch is accessed from the AWS console, and how our actions from the previous sections appear in the AWS console.

CloudWatch in the AWS console

CloudWatch is also now available in the AWS console in its detailed form.

1. To access CloudWatch, click on the **CloudWatch** tab in the AWS console:

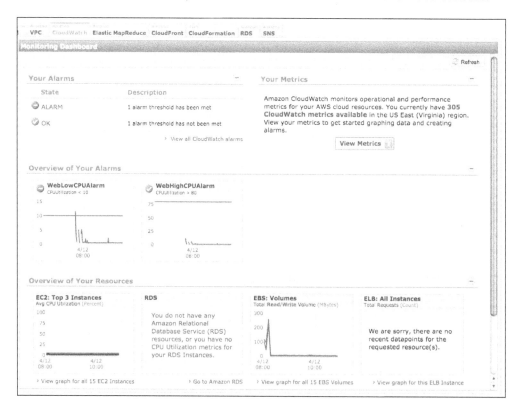

The first thing you may notice is that there are already two alarms specified, those we specified for our autoscaling web group (WebLowCLUAlarm and WebHighCPUAlarm). One thing I didn't cover in the previous section was that once an autoscaling group has been created along with the relevant policies, these can be managed from within the AWS console.

2. To demonstrate this, let's create a new alarm that sends an SNS alert when the AppAutoScaleGroup falls below 10 percent for more than 120 seconds. To start this process, click on the **View all CloudWatch alarms** link in the **Your Alarms** section, as shown in the previous screenshot. This will take you to the **Your CloudWatch Alarms** page:

3. Click on the **Create Alarm** button to create a new alarm and select the **Viewing** metrics drop-down combo. Select the **EC2: Aggregated by Auto Scaling Group** option:

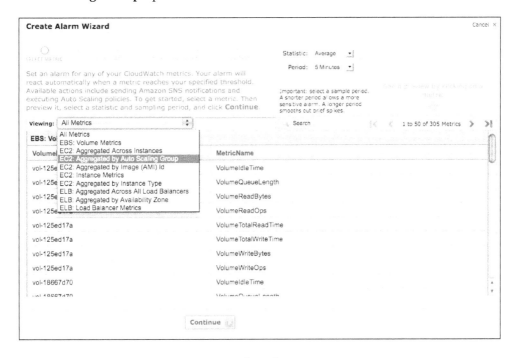

4. Select **CPUUtilization** as the **MetricName** and click **Continue**:

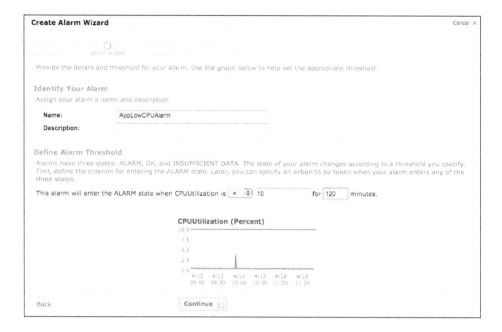

5. On the **Define Alarm** screen, enter a name for the alarm and the threshold and click on **Continue**. On the **Configure Actions** screen add an **Auto Scaling Policy** as one of the actions:

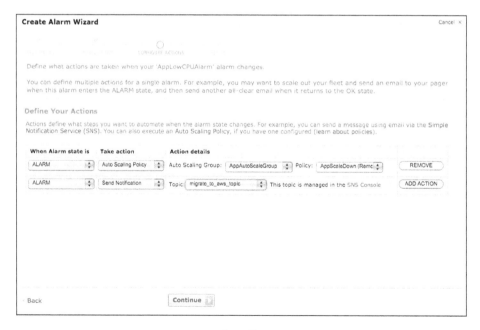

6. However, this time also add another action of **Send Notification** to the SNS topic we created in the previous chapter and click on **Continue**, and **Continue** again on the next summary screen. If we look at the alarms screen now, we should see the following:

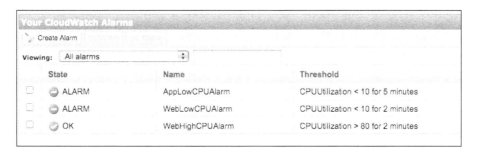

7. So, not only is this alarm controlling scaling down our application autoscale group, but when a scale down occurs, a message will be sent to the SNS group `migrate_to_aws_topic`. The following is a copy of the message that was sent from the SNS subscription when we triggered this alarm:

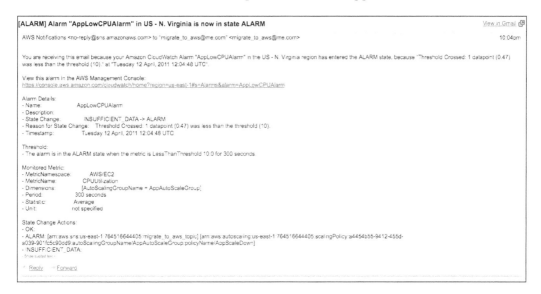

Pricing for CloudWatch

Pricing for CloudWatch is around $3.50 per instance per month, with a small extra cost for custom metrics of $0.50 per month.

Summary

In this chapter, we focussed on how we can use **Amazon Cloud Watch** and **Amazon Auto Scaling** to add flexibility to our sample application Waaah. We implemented an autoscale group for both our web servers and application servers to allow our sample application to scale from two to four web servers and two to four application servers when the average CPU of the existing servers stayed above 80 percent for 120 seconds. Our **Amazon Load Balancers** handled the routing transparently and the implementation of **Amazon Simple Notification Service** alerts notified us of when autoscaling events occurred.

So now we have a flexible scalable implementation of our Waaah application with notification and performance monitoring built-in!

In the next chapter, we will be looking at how to test and maintain our application when it is hosted up on AWS.

10
Testing and Maintaining the Application

In this chapter, we will be looking at how we operationally support our application once it has been migrated to AWS. We will look at load testing, patch management, backups, and management of quality assurance environments.

Post deployment

If you have been working in the IT industry for a while, you will no doubt be aware that the post deployment period of an application can be a stressful period in the project lifecycle. This is the critical time when your new application is used by a large group of users outside of the sanitized testing environment for the first time. To ensure that you get through this period as effortlessly as possible, I recommend that you invest the time in ensuring that you have the areas mentioned above well and truly covered in advance.

Of these areas, the one (in my experience) that has caused utmost pain in post deployment is performance, performance, and performance. Finding out that a brand new application suddenly starts performing poorly when deployed to its user base is something that I have seen over and over again for the past 20 years in Information Technology. I cannot stress enough the importance of **Load Testing** as an important step in the deployment and post deployment process. So for the first part of this chapter, I will be focusing on load testing!

Load testing

Load Testing is designed to place an application under a load that is repeatable and scalable and that emulates a real world use case of the application. Setting up an environment (including test data) can be a time-consuming task, and one which is often done poorly.

 The key words in the previous paragraph are 'repeatable' and 'scalable'. It is these two items, in conjunction with ensuring that the use case is relevant, which ensure that the performance is tested adequately.

There are many vendors and applications, that provide load test services and applications. However, as has been the goal throughout this book, I will use an actual example that you will be able to follow yourself. The example I will be using is **Grinder**, a popular open source load test framework that has been implemented handily into an Amazon AMI already for us.

Grinder—an open source load test tool

To start with Grinder, I recommend that you download and read the documentation located at the Grinder AMI page on AWS: `http://aws.amazon.com/amis/2055`.

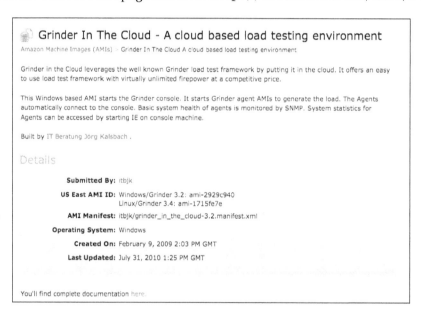

However, if you just want to get started, follow the steps mentioned next:

Starting the AMI

Before starting the Grinder AMI, you will need to create a new security group called "**All Incoming**". Once this group is created add the following ports:

TCP Port (Service)	Source
22 (SSH)	0.0.0.0/0
80 (HTTP)	0.0.0.0/0
3389 (RDP)	0.0.0.0/0
6372	0.0.0.0/0
UDP Port (Service)	**Source**
161	0.0.0.0/0

 The password for this AMI has already been set, so you will not need to use a key pair.

Once the ports have been added, start the AMI (**ami-2929c940**) in the **US-EAST** region and make sure that this security group has been added on start up.

 The Grinder AMI for Windows is ami-2929c940 and is only available in the US-EAST region.

Once the Grinder EC2 instance has been started, connect to it with RDP using the following credentials, which are provided in the Grinder documentation:

Username: **Administrator**

Password: **NmD1M2czuV**

Using grinder

When you first log in to the Grinder EC2 instance, you will be greeted with the following screen:

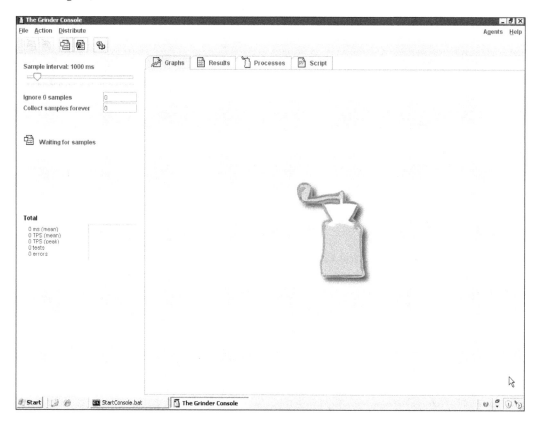

As you can see, Grinder is executed for you automatically when you log in. Now we are ready to start.

There are a few steps required to use grinder.

1. Modify the registry values on all of your servers
2. Start the remote agents
3. Creating/Editing the test scripts
4. Running the test

Modifying the registry values on all of your servers

Before running any load test in a Windows environment, there are some registry settings that we will need to change. The first registry change increases the number of ports from the default of 5000 to 65534. The second registry change decreases the time to wait before closing a previously used socket, as it is possible to run out of sockets if a high number of connections are received per second.

HKLM\System\CurrentControlSet\Services\Tcpip\Parameters\MaxUserPort = 0xfffe

HKLM\System\CurrentControlSet\Services\Tcpip\Parameters\ TcpTimedWaitDelay = 0x2

These settings will need to be changed on the web servers and are both DWORD values.

 The web servers will need to be rebooted after these registry changes have been made.

Starting the remote agents

As with most load testing utilities, the load test is carried out by one or more 'agents', controlled by a 'controller'. In this case, the controller is the Grinder console that you see in front of you, and the agents will be new EC2 instances started by Grinder.

 These are standard EC2 instances and you will be charged at regular EC2 rates for these.

The new EC2 instances will automatically shut down when you log out of the grinder console, or log off the RDP session. However, if you disconnect from the RDP session or kill the grinder console from task manager, the EC2 agents will need to be shut down manually.

For this session, we will be starting two Grinder agents. We will need two agents, as our **AWS Load Balancer** has been set to use 'Sticky' sessions, which means that connections from an agent will be directed back to the same web server by the load balancer. So two agents should load balance across two web servers quite nicely.

1. To start the agents click on the **Agents** menu option on the right of the Grinder Console window:

2. You will need to enter your access key as well as your secret access key, along with the number of agents that you would like to start:

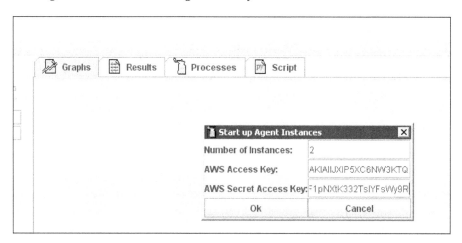

3. To check on the status of your new agents, click on the **Processes** tab at the top of the Grinder Console. You should see the two agents running:

4. If you switch to your AWS Console, you will also see the two new agent EC2 instances running:

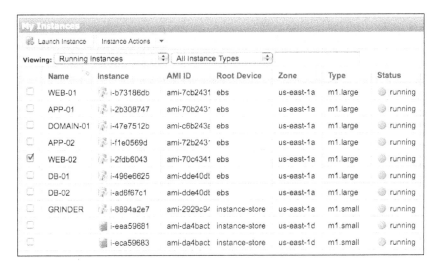

Now that we have our agents running, it's time to configure our test script.

Creating/Editing the test scripts

For our test we won't be creating a new test script but will be modifying an existing test script in the examples. To start, click on the **Script** tab at the top of the screen and expand the file tree on the left-hand side:

As you can see, there are two files highlighted with yellow stars. The file **grinder. properties** is the main bootstrap file, which is used to control the Grinder tests. So go ahead and double-click on it, it should open for editing in the right-hand windowpane.

Most of the options in this file are commented out. However, there are two important options that you should be aware of:

```
grinder.script = http.py
```

This sets the test script to be used when running tests; by default it is set to **http.py** (the other script with a yellow star against it).

```
Grinder.threads = 10
```

This sets the number of threads that will execute the test script on each agent machine. For our test example, we will leave both of these alone, as we will be modifying the **http.py** script to suit our own requirements.

Now that we've had a look at the main Grinder controller script, let's open up the **http.py** script by double-clicking on it:

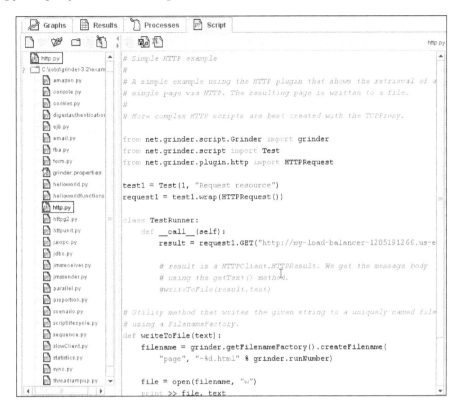

We will be changing only two lines in this file. The first one would be to change the GET to the following:

```
Result = request1.GET("my-load-balancer-1205191266.us-east-
    1.elb.amazonaws.com")
```

Where the URL is the name of our load balancer for our web servers.

The second one is to comment out the following line:

```
#writeToFile(result.text)
```

As we do not want to write the contents of our GET to the filesystem.

Running the test

Now that we have configured everything that we need, we are ready to run the test. However, there are a couple of things to be aware of first:

- The first thing to be aware of is that our AWS load Balancer will automatically throttle our load test after about 40 seconds. So only run the test for 30 seconds.

- The second thing to be aware of is that for this test we are only testing the performance of the home page of our website, we are not testing the performance of either our WCF web service or our database server.

 The AWS Load Balancer will automatically throttle our load test after around 40 seconds, as it believes it is under a **Denial of Service (DoS)** attack.

To run the test, first click on the **Start Collecting Statistics** button:

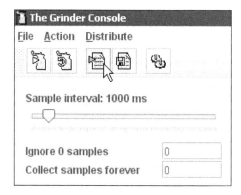

Then click on the **Start the Worker Processes** button:

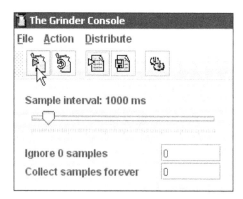

At this point you may be asked to update the cache on the worker processes, select **yes** as the changes to the scripts will now need to be propagated out to our two agent servers.

Immediately, you will see things begin to happen. On the front screen, you will see the number of tests that were executed each second as well as the mean and peak number. On the **Processes** tab, you will see the threads start up and display under each agent.

After 30 seconds, click on the **Reset the Worker Processes** button. In my test, I was able to achieve a throughput of around 1000 TPS:

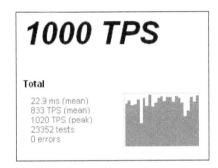

Re-running the test

That's it, you should now be able to use the previous information to create more complex tests, but we are not quite finished yet. To truly load test our infrastructure, we need to test what happens when we scale out our web servers!

To re-run this test, let's double the number of web servers by bundling up one of our existing web servers and using the resultant AMI to launch two new instances. (Making sure they are in the **Web Servers** security group).

If you need a refresh on how to do this, we covered bundling and creating new AMIs in *Chapter 3, Getting Started with AWS and Amazon EC2.*

After we have launched them, we will need to manually add them to our existing web load balancer so that we now have four web servers running behind our load balancer.

Our running EC2 instances should now resemble the following screenshot:

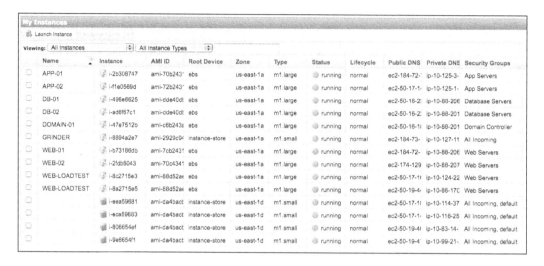

Just to summarize the running instances we have:

1. Two application servers (APP-01, APP-02)

2. Two database servers (DB-01, DB-02)

3. A domain controller (DOMAIN-01)

4. The Grinder Controller (GRINDER)

5. Four web servers (WEB-01, WEB-02, WEB-LOADTEST x 2)

6. Four Grinder agents (unnamed)

So let's re-run the Grinder load test and see what happens. (I have added another two Grinder agents to cater for the extra two web servers).

The results are:

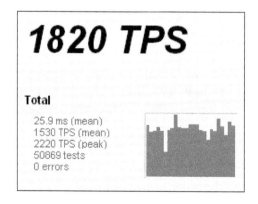

As you can see from the results, our peak **Tests Per Second (TPS)** increased from 1020 TPS to 2220 TPS, and our average TPS increased from 833 TPS to 1530 TPS!

Patch Management, Quality Assurance (QA), and backups

Now that we have covered off load testing, it's time to look at **Patch Management**, **Quality Assurance (QA)**, and **backups**, all of which are related.

One of the major issues with the management of production applications is the management of day-to-day issues, such as releases of new versions, creation of test environments and testing, and application of patches. These are usually limited by the availability of hardware and the availability of up-to-date environments for testing. However, with AWS we have a tremendous advantage; we no longer need to wait for hardware to be provisioned or environments to be created!

Using our backups from our database server in conjunction with the ability to bundle live production instances, we have all the tools we need to create exact duplicates of the production environment at any time.

Let's look at how we would use this in a production environment.

The problem to be solved

For our example, let's pretend for the minute that we have been asked by our organization to ensure that the production environment is fully updated with all service packs and updates. Normally, (depending on the organization) we would be asked to apply these to the QA test environment prior to being applied to production. However, our test environments tend to be populated with new releases coming up into production, so unless we have a dedicated production copy specifically set aside for this purpose, our testing of patches will be undertaken against not the current release in production, but the next release coming into production. We also need to make sure that performance is not impacted, so it would be advantageous to have an exact copy of the same hardware used in the current production environment.

The solution

In AWS, we have a solution to this and other related problems, which is both elegant and provides for a full rollback in the event of any issues as well as allowing full load and performance to be undertaken. In the next sections, I will cover the step-by-step process by which this is possible in AWS.

Solving the problem, step-by-step

The solution that we are going to follow will proceed with the following steps:

- Bundle the production EC2 instances to AMI images (WEB-01, WEB-02, APP-01, APP-02, DB-01, DB-02, and DOMAIN-01).

- Create new running EC2 instances from these AMIs.

- Configure the new instances.

- Apply the relevant patches and service packs.

- Re-run the functional tests.

- Re-run the grinder load test.

As you can see from the previous list, there are quite a few steps involved. However, they are not complex and can be completed readily. For steps that have been completed in previous chapters, you will be referred to those chapters instead of detailing the steps again.

Bundling the existing production EC2 instances

Bundling running EC2 instances was covered in *Chapter 3, Getting Started with AWS and Amazon EC2*, so it won't be covered here. However, make sure you give each bundled AMI a name which you will recognize. In this example, I have used the following names.

Production Instance Name	Bundled AMI Name
WEB-01	WEB-01-QA
WEB-02	WEB-02-QA
APP-01	APP-01-QA
APP-02	APP-02-QA
DB-01	DB-01-QA
DB-02	DB-02-QA
DOMAIN-01	DOMAIN-01-QA

Creating new running EC2 instances

Before we create our new EC2 instances, we will need to create four new security groups. Initially, the only access granted to these groups will be RDP; this will ensure that we can't accidentally connect to the production instance. So go ahead and create the following security groups.

New Security Groups	Port Access
Web Servers (Environment 02)	RDP Only
App Servers (Environment 02)	RDP Only
Database Servers (Environment 02)	RDP Only
Domain Controller 02 (Environment 02)	RDP Only

Now start up and name each instance (using AWS Tags) as follows:

New Security Groups	New EC2 Instances
Web Servers (Environment 02)	WEB-03, WEB-04
App Servers (Environment 02)	APP-03, APP-04
Database Servers (Environment 02)	DB-03, DB-04
Domain Controller 02 (Environment 02)	DOMAIN-02

Configuring the new instances

Now that we have our new instances up and running, we need to configure them before we allow them access outside of their restricted security group.

Allocating a new elastic IP addresses and modifying the DNS settings

Allocate an elastic IP address to the new domain controller (DOMAIN-02) and the new primary database server (DB-03).

Now RDP to DB-03 and modify the DNS server in the network configuration to point to the IP address of the new Domain Controller.

In our example, the new elastic IP addresses are:

EC2 Instance Name	IP address	Public DNS
DOMAIN-02	184.73.223.216	ec2-184-73-223-216.compute-1.amazonaws.com
DB-03	184.73.175.58	ec2-184-73-175-58.compute-1.amazonaws.com

So the new DNS entry would be set to 184.73.223.216:

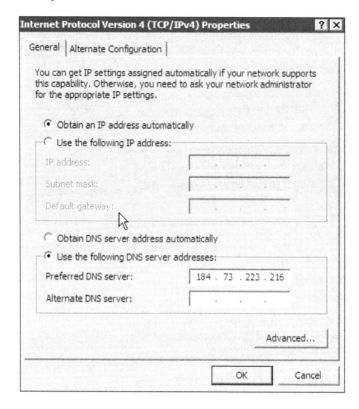

Creating new load balancers

The next step is to create the two new load balancers for the new environment.

So go ahead and create one for the new web servers (WEB-03 and WEB-04) and one for the new application servers (APP-03 and APP-04). At this point, the status will point to both instances being out of service, but that will be resolved when we finish this configuration step.

Modifying the web.config files

The next step is to modify the `web.config` file on WEB-03 and WEB-04 with the new configuration changes.

 It is important to modify the entire configuration files prior to allowing the servers access outside of their restricted security groups.

You will need to modify the **web.config** in the same three locations as documented in *Chapter 7, Migrating your Data and Deploying your Code*, the two database locations **WidgetEntities** and **ApplicationServices**, should be changed to point to the Public DNS of **DB-03**, and the client WCF endpoint at the end of the **web.config**, should be modified to point to the new application load balancer.

Modifying the security groups

Now that we have changed the configuration files and created the new load balancers, we can allow the servers to see one another via their security groups.

Modify the **Domain Controllers (Environment 02)** security group to allow access from both the **Database Servers (Environment 02)** group as well as the elastic IP address allocated to DB-03 for both UDP and TCP/IP:

ICMP	
Port (Service)	**Source**
ALL	184.73.175.58/32
TCP	
Port (Service)	**Source**
1 - 65535	184.73.175.58/32
1 - 65535	sg-10422979 (Database Servers (Environment 02))
3389 (RDP)	0.0.0.0/0
UDP	
Port (Service)	**Source**
1 - 65535	184.73.175.58/32
1 - 65535	sg-10422979 (Database Servers (Environment 02))

 You will find that the database will not start initially because it has been configured with domain service accounts; once you have allowed access through to the domain controller, the database services will be able to start.

The next step is to allow access to DB-03 from the web servers. So modify the **Database Servers (Environment 02)** security group to allow access from the web servers. Allow access on port 1433:

TCP	
Port (Service)	**Source**
1433 (MS SQL)	sg-00422969 (Web Servers (Environment 02))
3389 (RDP)	0.0.0.0/0

Finally, modify the **Application Servers (Environment 02)** security group and **Web Servers (Environment 02)** security group to allow access from everyone on port 80:

TCP Port (Service)	Source
3389 (RDP)	0.0.0.0/0
80 (HTTP)	0.0.0.0/0

We now have a duplicate production environment up and running in Environment 02!

So our setup now looks like the following diagram. It is an exact copy barring any changes in data in our database:

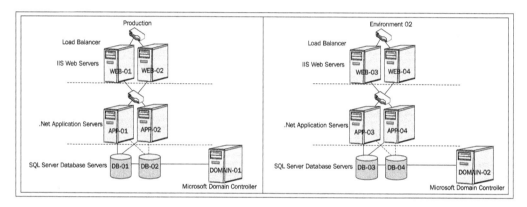

Now we are ready to apply our service packs and patches required for testing.

It is worthwhile noting that the time to duplicate the entire production environment for our sample application Waaah was **47 minutes**! Wow!

Applying the relevant patches and service packs

I'll leave it up to your imagination what you would do in this step. However, for the purposes of this exercise, I did actually install all of the outstanding service packs and updates for all of the servers within our new environment (Environment 02) just to prove a point.

 It is also probably worth noting that the entire update process took over three hours for all of the servers when I undertook it for this exercise.

Re-running the functional tests

Now that we have installed the service packs and the updates, it's time to re-run any functional tests to ensure that we didn't break our application Waaah. Because Waaah is a fairly simple application a quick once through was enough to show that all was operating as expected.

Re-run the Grinder load test

To re-run the Grinder load test on our new environment, all we need to do is edit the **http.py** script and change the address from the load balancer on our production environment to the new load balancer on our new environment. For those of you who are interested, re-running the Grinder load test on our new environment after installing all of the latest updates resulted in the following stats:

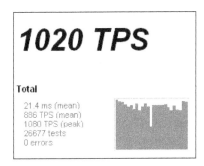

Overall, there was a slight increase in performance; however, the increase was within 10 percent, so is deemed not significant!

The solution for the next steps

Now that we have thoroughly tested our patches and updates through a QA environment, that is, an exact duplicate of the production environment and passed both the functional testing and the load testing, there is the question of what to do for the next steps.

We currently have two environments. One environment is fully patched, tested and up to date, however, the database is full of test data. The other environment has the correct production data, but will require an outage of at least three hours to update all of the servers.

In the past, it hasn't been feasible to do what I am about to suggest, but with the capability of AWS at our fingertips, what was difficult for many reasons yesterday, is simple today.

Now that we have passed our new environment through our testing, why not migrate it to production and demote the existing production environment?

There are some advantages to doing it this way:

- The time to migrate the production database to the new environment will be quite fast if we migrate the EBS volumes directly from the old production database to the new production database.
- There is a fast rollback plan in play ready to go if issues crept through the testing process.
- The total outage time for our environment will be in total, less than ten minutes, or the time taken to detach and re-attach the EBS volumes from production.

Updating the original production environment has the following disadvantages:

- The rollback plan at best will require the restarting of production servers from AMI bundled images.
- The update process will require three hours, of which a substantial amount of time may be offline.

So well worth thinking about.

Summary

In this chapter, we got a detailed look at how we can perform load testing on our AWS enterprise application by using a Grinder Amazon Machine Image (AMI). We saw the step-by-step process of how we can use Grinder to test our application, and how to modify it to cater for increased infrastructure requirements.

We also got a detailed look at how we can use the features of AWS to perform day-to-day production activities such as implementing new releases and patch/update management into QA environments.

In the last section, we saw that we could start with a running production environment, create a copy in under an hour, and re-run all of the functional and load testing on an exact copy of the hardware being used in production.

In my humble opinion, that's amazing! All for the cost of less than $10/day per server, or in the case of our sample application, it's less than $100/day.

This is the final chapter of our ride together, and I hope you enjoyed it. I've taken you from the very beginning of having an application running in your enterprise, to having the same application running in the cloud.

Along the way, we have looked at a large part (but not all) of the functionality provided by AWS and I have been constantly amazed at how much has changed while I have been writing this book.

AWS Reference

List of AWS terms and keywords

Keywords are documented in the chapter sections in order where they are first
mentioned and are not repeated in the later sections of the chapter. If you are unable
to find the keyword that you are looking for in the relevant chapter section, please
check the chapter sections prior to the one you are looking in.

Chapter 1

- **Amazon Web Services (AWS)**: A collection of services provided by Amazon
  supplying computer resources on demand:

  http://aws.amazon.com

- **.Net**: A runtime framework written by Microsoft to allow sophisticated
  applications to be developed similar to Java by running them on a runtime
  virtual machine:

  http://www.microsoft.com/net

- **Load Balancing**: The practice of allocating TCP/IP connections in a round
  robin fashion to an array of web servers to ensure that HTTP requests are
  balanced evenly across all of the servers:

  http://aws.amazon.com/elasticloadbalancing

- **Virtual Private Network (VPN)**: A network that is private and cordoned
  off from general IP traffic. This is achieved by encrypting traffic before it is
  passed over public TCP/IP connections that are shared by other users, such
  as the Internet:

  http://en.wikipedia.org/wiki/Virtual_private_network

- **Amazon Simple Queue Service (SQS)**: A service provided by Amazon to allow asynchronous, reliable queuing, and retrieval of messages:

  `http://aws.amazon.com/sqs`

- **Simple Notification Services (SNS)**: A service provided by Amazon to allow event notification and alerting to multiple subscribers:

  `http://aws.amazon.com/sns`

- **.ASP .Net**: A version of .Net specifically designed for the implementation of websites:

  `http://www.asp.net`

- **.ASP Model View Controller** or **(MVC)**: A version of .Net specifically designed for the implementation of websites that follow the model, view, controller implementation and design pattern:

  `http://www.asp.net/mvc`

- **Microsoft SQL Server**: An enterprise class SQL database provided by Microsoft:

  `http://www.microsoft.com/sql`

- **C# .NET**: A specific version of .Net to allow the use of C#, a safe derivative of C and C++. C# was developed by Microsoft and is proprietary to Microsoft:

  `http://msdn.microsoft.com/en-us/vcsharp/aa336706`

- **Microsoft's Internet Information Server (IIS)**: An enterprise class web server provided by Microsoft:

  `http://www.iis.net`

- **Microsoft Active Directory (AD)**: An enterprise class authentication and security framework provided by Microsoft:

  `http://www.microsoft.com/windowsserver2008/en/us/ad-main.aspx`

- **Infrastructure as a Service (IaaS)**: A classification used to cover all web services that provide the lowest form of service, such as virtual servers, networks, and storage:

  `http://en.wikipedia.org/wiki/Infrastructure_as_a_service#Infrastructure`

- **Platform as a Service (PaaS)**: A classification used to cover services, which are more complex than IaaS such as hosted database solutions or hosted web solutions:

  http://en.wikipedia.org/wiki/Platform_as_a_service

- **Software as a Service (SaaS)**: A classification used to cover services, which are in effect complete applications such as Salesforce.com:

  http://en.wikipedia.org/wiki/Software_as_a_service

- **Microsoft's Azure**: A competitor to AWS developed by Microsoft with emphasis on hosting the .Net runtime in the cloud:

  http://www.microsoft.com/windowsazure

- **Google's App Engine**: A PaaS solution developed by Google for hosting applications in the Google cloud:

  http://code.google.com/appengine

- **Microsoft Office Live**: A SaaS solution provided by Microsoft for hosting Microsoft Office in the cloud:

  http://www.officelive.com

- **SAS70 Type II audit**: A classification of security audit that focuses on accountability and security of sensitive data:

  http://aws.amazon.com/about-aws/whats-new/2009/11/11/aws-completes-sas70-type-ii-audit

- **Elastic Block Store (EBS)**: A service provided by Amazon that provisions raw disk to Amazon EC2 instances:

  http://aws.amazon.com/ebs

- **Public Cloud**: Cloud services, which are made available to the general public:

  http://en.wikipedia.org/wiki/Cloud_computing

- **Virtual Private Cloud (VPC)**: Cloud services, which are segmented or isolated from the general public:

  http://aws.amazon.com/vpc

Chapter 2

- **AWS EC2 console**: The web console provided by Amazon to manage many functions from within AWS:

  https://console.aws.amazon.com

- **Simple Storage Service (S3)**: An object store provided by Amazon that allows the storage of arbitrary objects in the cloud:

  http://aws.amazon.com/s3

- **S3 Bucket**: The top-level location defined within S3 that will hold all objects stored. S3 buckets must be uniquely named:

  http://aws.amazon.com/s3/#getting-started

- **S3 Prefix**: The equivalent to a namespace that further defines where an object is stored in S3:

  http://aws.amazon.com/s3/#getting-started

- **Service Level Agreement (SLA)**: An agreement that defines what services will be provided at what quality and over what period. A SLA is not normally a sales contract but is used mainly to provide information on the level of service a web service will be provided at:

  http://en.wikipedia.org/wiki/Service_level_agreement

- **Reduced Redundancy Storage**: A type of S3 storage that has fewer copies stored for redundancy, and is therefore cheaper to use:

  http://aws.amazon.com/s3

- EC2 '**bundle**': A copy of a running EC2 instance, which can be used to start up other instances:

- **Amazon Machine Image (AMI)**: Similar to a Bundle, an AMI is used as the base to start up new machine instances in EC2:

- **Remote Desktop Protocol (RDP)**: A protocol developed by Microsoft to allow the remote control of server desktops:

  http://support.microsoft.com/kb/186607

- Ec2 '**Terminated**': Used to refer to an EC2 instance which when shut down is destroyed:

- Ec2 '**stop**': Used to refer to an EC2 instance which when shut down is not destroyed and may be started up again:

- **Amazon EC2 Request Form**: Used to request unusual services from Amazon. An example would be requiring more than five Elastic IP Addresses or more than 20 running EC2 instances:

  `http://aws.amazon.com/contact-us/ec2-request`

- **Key Pair**: Refers to a public/private key pair used by Amazon to secure access to AWS resources.

- **Elastic IP**: A static IP address allocated by Amazon and guaranteed never to change for the lifetime of owning it. Currently limited to five per region:

  `http://aws.amazon.com/ec2/faqs/#Why_am_I_limited_to_5_Elastic_IP_addresses`

- **Reserved Instance**: An instance that is reserved in advance which guarantees access to pre-allocated resources when requested:

  `http://aws.amazon.com/ec2/reserved-instances`

- **Spot instances**: Instances that are requested when there is extra availability. Usually costs less than a normal instance:

  `http://aws.amazon.com/ec2/spot-instances`

- **High Performance Compute** (**HPC**): Used by Amazon to refer to a class of EC2 instance that has either very high network connectivity or powerful graphics accelerators:

  `http://aws.amazon.com/ec2/hpc-applications`

- **Storage Area Network** (**SAN**): A network connected to a device which supplies disk storage. Can be either fiber optic or copper:

  `http://en.wikipedia.org/wiki/Storage_area_network`

- **Windows Perfmon**: An application developed by Microsoft to display Windows WMI counters:

- **Windows Management Instrumentation** (**WMI**): A framework developed by Microsoft to supply events and alerting from running Windows instances:

  `http://msdn.microsoft.com/en-us/library/aa394582%28v=vs.85%29.aspx`

- **Amazon Relational Database Service** (**RDS**): A hosted MySQL service provided by Amazon:

  `http://aws.amazon.com/rds`

- **Multi-AZ Deployments**: Used in reference to RDS and describes a RDS configuration where there are multiple copies of MySQL running in different availability zones:

  `http://aws.amazon.com/about-aws/whats-new/2010/05/18/`
  `announcing-multi-az-deployments-for-amazon-rds/`

- **Read Replica**: A copy of the database that is read only. Often used for reporting purposes.

Chapter 3

- **Sysprep:** A utility provided by Microsoft to allow the modification of an existing Windows server to be copied whilst ensuring that things such as security information and the internal SSID are deleted or modified:

  `http://en.wikipedia.org/wiki/Sysprep`

- **VMware Tools**: The tools provided by VMware that are installed on virtual machines running in a VMware infrastructure environment:

  `http://www.vmware.com/support/ws55/doc/ws_newguest_tools_`
  `windows.html`

- **System Identifier** (SSID): The internal identifier used by Windows to uniquely identify itself on the network. Infamously, no two Windows servers with the same SSID may be connected to the same Domain Controller:

- **Windows Domain Controlle**r: A server developed by Microsoft to handle security and authentication in the enterprise:

  `http://en.wikipedia.org/wiki/Domain_controller`

- **Sysprep answer file**: A file used to provide pre-canned answers to the Sysprep program.

- **AMI ID**: The unique ID given to an Amazon Machine Image or bundle.

- **Instance ID**: The unique ID given to a running EC2 machine instance.

Chapter 4

- **S3 Access Key**: A key provided by Amazon and used to secure access to AWS resources. Normally used in conjunction with a Secret Access Key.

- **S3 Secret Access Key**: A secret key (similar to a password) used to authenticate to AWS resources. Normally used in conjunction with an Access Key.

- **S3Fox**: A Firefox plugin which enables users to access S3 from inside a browser:

  `http://www.s3fox.net`

- **Tag Name**: An optional name that may be allocated to certain AWS resources, such as EC2 instances and EBS disks.

Chapter 5

- **Tracert**: A program used to trace the TCP/IP route that is taken by a packet to get to its destination:

  `http://en.wikipedia.org/wiki/Traceroute`

- **Cmd Prompt**: The Dos prompt in Windows.

- **Microsoft Data Access Components (MDAC 2.6)**: A series of components developed by Microsoft to allow access to various database technologies:

  `http://msdn.microsoft.com/en-us/library/ms810805.aspx`

Chapter 6

- **SimpleDB:** A service provided by Microsoft that allows simple key/value storage in the cloud:

  `http://aws.amazon.com/simpledb`

- **On-Demand**: An on-demand instance is an instance that has requested adhoc from the AWS EC2 pool. Other types of instances are 'reserved' and 'spot' instances.

- **Mixed Mode Security**: A security mode used by SQL Server to allow both Microsoft Domain authentication as well as direct SQL Server authentication.

- **Internet Explorer Enhanced Security Configuration**: A security configuration enabled by default, which prevents the use of a web browser for most tasks on a Windows server:

  `http://technet.microsoft.com/en-us/library/dd883248%28WS.10%29.aspx`

- **SSH:** A secure shell protocol, which uses encrypted communications between the client and the server:

  `http://en.wikipedia.org/wiki/Secure_Shell`

- **PuTTY:** A freeware program that implements the SSH protocol:

  `http://www.chiark.greenend.org.uk/~sgtatham/putty/`

- **Enterprise Manager** (**EM**): The name of the application used by Oracle to manage resources once a database has been installed.

- **MySQL**: An open source relational database now owned by Oracle:

  http://www.mysql.com

- **Mysqldump**: A utility used with MySQL to back up data as required:

  http://dev.mysql.com/doc/refman/5.1/en/mysqldump.html

- **Mysql Shell**: The command-line program used to access MySQL features:

  http://dev.mysql.com/doc/refman/5.5/en/mysql.html

Chapter 7

- Visual Web Developer 2010 Express: A development suite provided by Microsoft to allow the development of web applications in the .Net framework:

  http://www.microsoft.com/express/Web

- Forms Security: A security model used for authentication where authentication is managed by the application:

  http://www.asp.net/security/tutorials/an-overview-of-forms-authentication-vb

- SQL Server Mirroring: A term used to describe the implementation of a database such that it has a copy offline, which is kept up-to-date in the event of failure of the original database:

  http://msdn.microsoft.com/en-us/library/ms189852.aspx

- Windows Communication Foundation (WCF): A framework developed by Microsoft that encapsulates communication methods and protocols:

  http://msdn.microsoft.com/en-us/netframework/aa663324

Chapter 8

- **SQS Scratchpad**: The utility provided by Amazon that allows the testing of SQS API elements:

  http://aws.amazon.com/code/1254

- **AWS SDK for .Net**: A .Net library provided by Amazon to facilitate the implementation of .Net applications which use AWS resources:

  http://aws.amazon.com/sdkfornet

- **Software Development Kit (SDK)**: A generic description of anything that facilitates development.

- **Visibility Timeout**: Used in SQS and defines how long a message stays invisible after it has been read from the queue, but before it has been deleted.

- **Web Hooks**: A type of Web HTTP implementation, which allows third-party applications to call services remotely. An example of a site that demonstrates web hooks is:

  ```
  http://www.postbin.org
  ```

- **Topic**: Used in SNS and defines a namespace for notifications.

Chapter 9

- **AWS Autoscaling**: The ability for an infrastructure to dynamically increase or decrease the number of servers based on the demand:

  ```
  http://aws.amazon.com/autoscaling
  ```

- **CloudWatch**: A service provided by Amazon, which allows EC2 instances to provide alerts and statistics:

  ```
  http://aws.amazon.com/cloudwatch
  ```

- **Autoscaling Group**: A group of servers, which are treated with the same rules for scaling up or down.

- **Policy**: In Autoscaling, a policy defines the rules associated with an Autoscaling Group.

- **Amazon Resource Name (ARN)**: The internal unique name given to all Amazon resources. Not always visible.

Chapter 10

- **Load Testing**: A specific type of testing which artificially and repeatedly increases the load on an application:

  ```
  http://en.wikipedia.org/wiki/Load_testing
  ```

- **Grinder: An open source tool used to automate Load Testing:**

  ```
  http://grinder.sourceforge.net
  http://aws.amazon.com/amis/2055
  ```

- **Load Balancer 'Sticky'**: The term is used to define an AWS load balancer, which 'sticks' sessions to the same web server that they initiated contact on:

  http://aws.amazon.com/about-aws/whats-new/2010/04/08/support-for-session-stickiness-in-elastic-load-balancing

- **Denial of Service (DoS)**: A type of web attack that works by sending a large number of requests to an application in the hope that it will be swamped:

  http://en.wikipedia.org/wiki/Denial-of-service_attack

- **Tests Per Second (TPS)**: The number of tests that can be executed in a second.

- **Patch Management**: The process and policy of implementing patches onto production servers.

- **Quality Assurance (QA)**: A general term used to describe the quality of a service.

AWS products covered in this book

Here is a summary of the products covered in this book. Please note that this summary does not encompass all AWS products.

Amazon Elastic Compute Cloud (EC2)

EC2 provides virtual computing resources on demand, in effect allowing virtual servers to be spun up and down on demand in the AWS cloud.

Command-line tools

The command-line tools are provided by the Amazon staff and are located at:

http://aws.amazon.com/developertools/351

Environment variables used

These are the environment variables used when setting up command-line tools:

```
set JAVA_HOME="C:\Program Files\Java\jre6"
set EC2_PRIVATE_KEY=c:\aws\pk-XUSF3YX32DTZWSBHEIENR24EANXCXUBA.pem
set EC2_CERT=c:\aws\cert-XUSF3YX32DTZWSBHEIENR24EANXCXUBA.pem
set EC2_HOME=C:\AWS\ec2-api-tools\ec2-api-tools-1.3-62308
set PATH=%PATH%;C:\AWS\ec2-api-tools\ec2-api-tools-1.3-62308\bin
```

Commands used in the book:

These are the commands used in this book:

Command	Description	Chapter
`ec2-describe-regions`	List all of the current regions available	*Chapter 3, Getting Started with AWS and Amazon EC2*
`ec2-describe-images -o self`	List all of the AMIs owned by the AWS user	*Chapter 3, Getting Started with AWS and Amazon EC2*
`ec2-run-instances ami-70b24319 -g migrate_to_aws_ secure -k migrate_ to_aws_key_pair --availability-zone us-east-1a -monitor`	Start up an EC2 instance using AMI ami-70b24319 in the migrate_to_aws security group using the migrate_to_ aws_key_pair key pair in the us-east-1a availability zone	*Chapter 3, Getting Started with AWS and Amazon EC2*
`ec2-create-tags i-cc9b92a1 --tag "Name=DB01"`	Associate a tag with a running instance	*Chapter 3, Getting Started with AWS and Amazon EC2*
`ec2-describe- instances --filter "instance-state- name=running"`	Get a list of running instances	*Chapter 3, Getting Started with AWS and Amazon EC2*
`ec2-terminate- instances i-cc9b92a1`	Terminate a running instance	*Chapter 3, Getting Started with AWS and Amazon EC2*
`ec2-stop-instances i-cc9b92a1`	Stop a running instance	*Chapter 3, Getting Started with AWS and Amazon EC2*

The following figure shows the AWS console location for **EC2**:

Summary of instance types and costs

The following is a summary of the costs and types of instances:

Name	Description	Approximate cost/year
		(on demand Windows, not including storage, network or other AWS costs, costs are for comparison only and are in $US)
Standard – Small	1.7 GB RAM, 1 EC2 compute unit, 32 bit, 160 GB local storage	$1,051
Standard – Large	7.5 GB RAM, 4 EC2 compute units, 64 bit, 850 GB local storage	$4,204
Standard - Extra Large	15 GB RAM, 8 EC2 compute units, 64 bit, 1690 GB local storage	$8,409
Micro	613 MB RAM, variable EC2 compute units to a max of 2, 64 bit	$262
High Memory - Extra Large	17.1 GB RAM, 6.5 EC2 compute units, 64 bit, 420 GB local storage	$5,431
High Memory - Double Extra Large	32.4 GB RAM, 13 EC2 compute units, 850 GB local storage, 64 bit	$10,862
High Memory - Quadruple Extra Large	68.4 GB RAM, 26 EC2 compute units, 1690 GB local storage, 64 bit	$21,724
High CPU - Medium Instance	1.7 GB RAM, 5 EC2 compute units, 350Gb local storage, 16 bit	$2,540
High CPU - Extra Large	7 GB RAM, 20 EC2 compute units, 64 bit, 1690 GB local storage	$10,161

Amazon Simple Storage Service (S3)

S3 is an object store for storing files on the cloud in AWS. Files of up to five terabytes may be stored.

Command-line tools

S3 tools on Codeplex provided by third party.

Alternative tools provided at `s3tools.org` are located at:

`http://s3.codeplex.com`

To set up this tool use the following command:

`s3 auth <Access Key> <Secret Access Key>`

Commands used in the book

The following are the commands used throughout this book.

Command	Description	Chapter

`s3 auth`
`AKIAIIJXIP5XC6NW3KTQ`
`9UpktBlqDroY5C4Q7OnlF1pNX`
`tK332TslYFsWy9R`
	Set up credentials	*Chapter 4, How Storage Works on Amazon*

`s3 list`	List S3 buckets	*Chapter 4, How Storage Works on Amazon*
`s3 put migrate_to_aws_02` `myfile.txt`	Upload a file to S3	*Chapter 4, How Storage Works on Amazon*

`s3 put migrate_to_aws_02/`
`mybigfile/ mybigfile.txt /`
`big`
	Upload in chunks a large file to S3	*Chapter 4, How Storage Works on Amazon*

`s3 get migrate_to_aws_02/` `myfile.txt`	Download a file from S3	*Chapter 4, How Storage Works on Amazon*

`s3 get migrate_to_aws_02/`
`mybigfile/mybigfile.txt /`
`big`
	Download in chunks a big file from S3	*Chapter 4, How Storage Works on Amazon*

The following screenshot shows the AWS console location for **S3**:

Approximate costs

Storage for S3 costs approximately as follows:

For one (1) terabyte of storage for one year = $1,720

Amazon Elastic Block Store (EBS)

EBS provides raw disk to EC2 instances on AWS.

Command-line tools

Command-line tools are provided by the EC2 command-line tools package.

Commands used in the book:

These are the commands used throughout the book for EBS:

Command	Description	Chapter
`ec2-create-volume --size 20 --availability-zone us-east-1a`	Creates an EBS volume	*Chapter 4, How Storage Works on Amazon*
`ec2-attach-volume vol-b418c2dc -i i-e2fdea8f -d xvdg`	Attach an EBS volume	*Chapter 4, How Storage Works on Amazon*
`ec2-detach-volume vol-b418c2dc`	Detach an EBS volume	*Chapter 4, How Storage Works on Amazon*
`ec2-delete-volume vol-b418c2dc`	Delete an EBS volume	*Chapter 4, How Storage Works on Amazon*

Available EBS Devices

Windows: xvdf through to xvdp

Unix: /dev/sdf through to /dev/sdp

The following screenshot shows the AWS console location for EBS:

Approximate costs

Storage for EBS costs approximately as follows:

For one (1) terabyte of storage for one year = $1,228

Amazon Autoscaling

Amazon autoscaling provides for the dynamic creation of EC2 instances based on server demand.

Command-line tools

Autoscaling command-line tools are provided by Amazon staff.

The Autoscaling tools are located at:

http://aws.amazon.com/developertools/2535

The environment variables used for the autoscaling tools are:

```
set AWS_AUTO_SCALING_HOME=C:\AWS\AutoScaling-1.0.33.1
set PATH=C:\AWS\AutoScaling-1.0.33.1\bin;%PATH%
```

Commands used in the book:

These are the Autoscaling commands used throughout this book:

Command	Description	Chapter
`as-describe-launch-configs`	Describe launch configuration information	*Chapter 9, Monitoring and Scaling My Application*
`as-create-launch-config WebLaunchConfig --image-id ami-7cb54915 --instance-type m1.large -group "Web Servers"`	Create the autoscaling launch configuration	*Chapter 9, Monitoring and Scaling My Application*
`as-create-auto-scaling-group WebAutoScaleGroup --launch-configuration WebLaunchConfig --availability-zones us-east-1a --min-size 2 --max-size 4 -load-balancers my-load-balancer`	Create the autoscaling group	*Chapter 9, Monitoring and Scaling My Application*
`as-put-scaling-policy WebScaleUp --type ChangeInCapacity --adjustment 1 --cooldown 120 --auto-scaling-group WebAutoScaleGroup`	Create an autoscaling (scale up) policy	*Chapter 9, Monitoring and Scaling My Application*
`as-put-scaling-policy WebScaleDown --type ChangeInCapacity "--adjustment=-1" --cooldown 120 --auto-scaling-group WebAutoScaleGroup`	Create an autoscaling (scale down) policy	*Chapter 9, Monitoring and Scaling My Application*
`as-describe-auto-scaling-groups --headers`	List all of the autoscale groups	*Chapter 9, Monitoring and Scaling My Application*

There is no console access to Amazon Autoscaling.

Approximate costs

Amazon Autoscaling carries no additional fees for its use other than standard fees associated with EC2 instances, storage, and bandwidth.

Amazon CloudFront

Amazon CloudFront provides caching of website data in distributed locations worldwide to improve the performance of websites hosted in an AWS data center.

The following figure shows the AWS console location for **CloudFront**:

Approximate costs

The calculation for costs is complex and based on HTTP requests as well as the size of data transferred. However, as a rough guide:

One (1) TB of data transferred each month for the period of one year in the US region = $1,843.

Amazon SimpleDB

SimpleDB provides a simple key/value store for the reliable storage of simple data of any size.

Tools are located at

http://aws.amazon.com/code/1137

Development libraries are located at:

Language	Library Location
.Net	http://aws.amazon.com/sdkfornet/
Java	http://aws.amazon.com/sdkforjava/
PHP	http://aws.amazon.com/sdkforphp/
Ruby	http://aws.amazon.com/ruby/

There is no console access to Amazon SimpleDB.

Approximate costs

It is complex to approximate the cost for SimpleDB, however, as a rough guide:

One (1) TB of data stored in SimpleDB for a year will cost = $3,077.

If all of the data was transferred out in one year, data transfer cost = $1,843.

Amazon Relational Database Service (RDS)

RDS provides a MySQL instance running and managed by AWS.

Command-line tools

The command-line tools are provided by Amazon staff and are located at:

http://aws.amazon.com/developertools/2928

This is the only environment variable used:

`Set AWS_RDS_HOME`

The following screenshot shows the AWS console location for **RDS**:

Summary of instance types and costs:

Name	Description	Approximate Cost/year (on demand, costs include 1 TB of storage running for one year and are for comparison only and are in $US)
Small RDS Instance	1.7 GB RAM, 1 EC2 compute unit, moderate IO	$2,192
Large RDS Instance	7.5 GB RAM, 4 EC2 compute unit, high IO	$5,083
Extra Large RDS Instance	15 GB RAM, 8 EC2 compute units, high IO	$8,937
High Memory Extra Large RDS Instance	17.1 GB RAM, 6.5 EC2 compute units, high IO	$6,922

Name	Description	Approximate Cost/year
		(on demand, costs include 1 TB of storage running for one year and are for comparison only and are in $US)
High Memory Double Extra Large RDS Instance	34 GB RAM, 13 EC2 compute units, high IO	$12,616
High Memory Quadruple Extra Large RDS Instance	68 GB RAM, 26 EC2 compute units, high IO	$24,004

Amazon Simple Queue Service (SQS)

SQS provides for reliable asynchronous queuing and delivery of messages.

Command-line tools

The command-line tools are provided by Amazon staff.

The scratchpad is located at:

```
http://aws.amazon.com/code/1254
```

The .Net SDK is located at:

```
http://aws.amazon.com/sdkfornet/
```

There is no console access to Amazon SQS.

Approximate pricing

Pricing is $0.01 per 10,000 requests.

Amazon Simple Notification Service (SNS)

SNS provides for reliable event and notification delivery to multiple endpoints such as mail and HTTP.

Command-line tools

Amazon does not currently supply command-line tools for SNS.

Subscription options

- HTTPS
- HTTP
- E-mail
- E-mail (JSON)
- Amazon SQS

The following screenshot shows the AWS console location for **SNS**:

Approximate pricing

Pricing for one (1) TB of data transferred in/out of SNS every month over a twelve month period = $1,843

Amazon CloudWatch

CloudWatch provides monitoring and alerting of metrics within the EC2 AWS environment.

Command-line tools

The command-line tools are provided by Amazon staff.

The CloudWatch tools are located at:

```
http://aws.amazon.com/developertools/2534
```

The Cloudwatch environment variables used are:

```
set AWS_CLOUDWATCH_HOME=C:\AWS\CloudWatch-1.0.9.5
set PATH=C:\AWS\CloudWatch-1.0.9.5\bin;%PATH%
```

Commands used in the book:

The following are the commands for CloudWatch used throughout this book.

Command	Description	Chapter
`mon-describe-alarms`	Describe configured alarms	*Chapter 9, Monitoring and Scaling My Application*
`mon-put-metric-alarm WebHighCPUAlarm --comparison-operator GreaterThanThreshold --evaluation-periods 1 --metric-name CPUUtilization --namespace "AWS/ EC2" --period 120 --statistic Average --threshold 80 --alarm-actions arn:aws:autoscaling:us-east-1:764516644405:scalingPo licy:d3c53ac8-fa73-4cfd-9a06-a5f9d7e1a58f: autoScalingGroupName/ WebAutoScaleGroup:policyName/ WebScaleUp --dimensions "AutoScalingG roupName=WebAutoScaleGroup"`	Create the cloud watch metric	*Chapter 9, Monitoring and Scaling My Application*

The following screenshot shows the AWS console location for **CloudWatch**:

Approximate pricing

Pricing for monitoring one instance is $3.50/month.

Amazon Virtual Private Cloud (VPC)

VPC allows the creation of custom, isolated compute environments with custom IP addressing schemes and isolated security.

Command-line tools

Command-line tools are provided by the EC2 command-line tools package.

AWS console

The following screenshot shows the AWS console location for **VPC**:

Approximate pricing

Pricing for one VPC connection over a one year period is = $438.

Amazon Elastic Load Balancing

ELB provides TCP/IP load balancing across multiple EC2 instances.

Command-line tools

Command-line tools are provided by the EC2 command-line tools package.

The following screenshot shows the AWS console location for ELB:

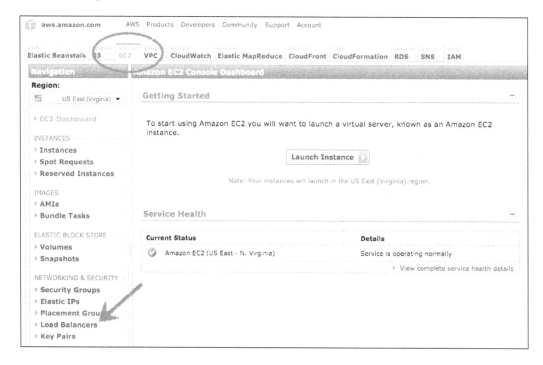

Approximate pricing

Pricing for one load balancer over a one year period if one (1) TB of data is transferred is = $317

Amazon Import/Export

Amazon import/export allows the transfer of large amounts of data in and out of AWS.

Command-line tools

The command-line tools are provided by Amazon staff and are located at:

`http://awsimportexport.s3.amazonaws.com/importexport-webservice-tool.zip`

Commands used in the book:

Command	Description	Chapter
`java -jar lib/ AWSImportExportWebServiceTool-1.0.jar CreateJob Import MyManifest.txt`	Create a job information	*Chapter 4, How Storage Works on Amazon*
`java -jar lib/ AWSImportExportWebServiceTool-1.0.jar ListJobs`	List all jobs	*Chapter 4, How Storage Works on Amazon*
`java -jar lib/ AWSImportExportWebServiceTool-1.0.jar CancelJob XHNHC`	Cancel a job	*Chapter 4, How Storage Works on Amazon*

There is no console access to Amazon SQS.

Approximate pricing

Around $80 per device

List of AWS data centers and regions

This is a list of AWS regions and availability zones:

- US East (Virginia)
    - us-east-1a
    - us-east-1b
    - us-east-1c
    - us-east-1d

- US West (North California)
    - us-west-1a
    - us-west-1b
    - us-west-1c

- EU West (Ireland)
    - eu-west-1a
    - eu-west-1b
    - eu-west-1c

- Asia Pacific (Singapore)
    - ap-southeast-1a
    - ap-southeast-1b

- Asia Pacific (Tokyo)
    - ap-northeast-1a
    - ap-northeast-1b

Location of CloudFront edge locations

The following is a list of the current CloudFront edge locations:

- United States
    - Ashburn, VA
    - Dallas/Fort Worth, TX
    - Jacksonville, FL
    - Los Angeles, CA

- ° Miami, FL
- ° New York, NY
- ° Newark, NJ
- ° Palo Alto, CA
- ° Seattle, WA
- ° St. Louis, MO

- Europe
  - ° Amsterdam
  - ° Dublin
  - ° Frankfurt
  - ° London
  - ° Paris

- Asia
  - ° Hong Kong
  - ° Tokyo
  - ° Singapore

Index

Symbols

A

F

G

weblog. *See* blog

webserver security group 47

Widgets are always available here. *See* Waaah

Windows Communication Foundation. *See* WCF

Windows Domain Controller 280

Windows Management Instrumentation. *See* WMI

Windows Perfmon 279

Windows Perfmon (The Microsoft performance monitoring tool) 54

WMI 54, 279

PUBLISHING

professional expertise distilled

Thank you for buying
Amazon Web Services: Migrating your
.NET Enterprise Application

About Packt Publishing

Packt, pronounced 'packed', published its first book "Mastering phpMyAdmin for Effective MySQL Management" in April 2004 and subsequently continued to specialize in publishing highly focused books on specific technologies and solutions.

Our books and publications share the experiences of your fellow IT professionals in adapting and customizing today's systems, applications, and frameworks. Our solution based books give you the knowledge and power to customize the software and technologies you're using to get the job done. Packt books are more specific and less general than the IT books you have seen in the past. Our unique business model allows us to bring you more focused information, giving you more of what you need to know, and less of what you don't.

Packt is a modern, yet unique publishing company, which focuses on producing quality, cutting-edge books for communities of developers, administrators, and newbies alike. For more information, please visit our website: www.packtpub.com.

About Packt Enterprise

In 2010, Packt launched two new brands, Packt Enterprise and Packt Open Source, in order to continue its focus on specialization. This book is part of the Packt Enterprise brand, home to books published on enterprise software – software created by major vendors, including (but not limited to) IBM, Microsoft and Oracle, often for use in other corporations. Its titles will offer information relevant to a range of users of this software, including administrators, developers, architects, and end users.

Writing for Packt

We welcome all inquiries from people who are interested in authoring. Book proposals should be sent to author@packtpub.com. If your book idea is still at an early stage and you would like to discuss it first before writing a formal book proposal, contact us; one of our commissioning editors will get in touch with you.

We're not just looking for published authors; if you have strong technical skills but no writing experience, our experienced editors can help you develop a writing career, or simply get some additional reward for your expertise.

Amazon SimpleDB Developer Guide

ISBN: 978-1-847197-34-4   Paperback: 252 pages

Scale your application's database on the cloud using Amazon SimpleDB with this book and eBook

1. Offload the time, effort, and capital associated with architecting and operating a simple, flexible, and scalable web database

2. A complete guide that covers everything from installation to advanced features aimed at optimizing your application

3. Examine SimpleDB and the relational database model and review the Simple DB data model

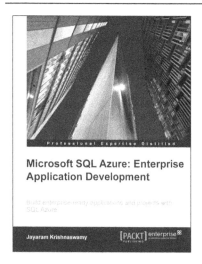

Microsoft SQL Azure Enterprise Application Development

ISBN: 978-1-849680-80-6   Paperback: 420 pages

Build enterprise-ready applications and projects with Microsoft SQL Azure using this book and eBook

1. Develop large scale enterprise applications using Microsoft SQL Azure

2. Understand how to use the various third party programs such as DB Artisan, RedGate, ToadSoft etc developed for SQL Azure

3. Master the exhaustive Data migration and Data Synchronization aspects of SQL Azure.

4. Includes SQL Azure projects in incubation and more recent developments including all 2010 updates

Please check **www.PacktPub.com** for information on our titles

Applied Architecture Patterns on the Microsoft Platform

ISBN: 978-1-849680-54-7   Paperback: 544 pages

An in-depth scenario-driven approach to architecting systems using Microsoft technologies with this book and eBook

1. Provides an architectural methodology for choosing Microsoft application platform technologies to meet the requirements of your solution

2. Examines new technologies such as Windows Server AppFabric, StreamInsight, and Windows Azure Platform and provides examples of how they can be used in real-world solutions

3. Considers solutions for messaging, workflow, data processing, and performance scenarios

Oracle Coherence 3.5

ISBN: 978-1-847196-12-5   Paperback: 408 pages

Create Internet-scale applications using Oracle's Coherence high-performance data grid with this book and eBook

1. Build scalable web sites and Enterprise applications using a market-leading data grid product

2. Design and implement your domain objects to work most effectively with Coherence and apply Domain Driven Designs (DDD) to Coherence applications

3. Leverage Coherence events and continuous queries to provide real-time updates to client applications

Please check **www.PacktPub.com** for information on our titles

www.ingramcontent.com/pod-product-compliance
Lightning Source LLC
LaVergne TN
LVHW062305060326

832902LV00013B/2058